Indrani Rengasamy

The Dialectics of Apartheid

D1826776

The art or practice of arriving at
the truth by the exchange of
logical arguments

The art of investigating or discussing the
truth of opinion.

Oxford Dictionary.

Indrani Rengasamy

The Dialectics of Apartheid

A Reading of Nadine Gordimer's Novels from a Postcolonial Perspective

LAP LAMBERT Academic Publishing

Impressum/Imprint (nur für Deutschland/ only for Germany)

Bibliografische Information der Deutschen Nationalbibliothek: Die Deutsche Nationalbibliothek verzeichnet diese Publikation in der Deutschen Nationalbibliografie; detaillierte bibliografische Daten sind im Internet über http://dnb.d-nb.de abrufbar.

Alle in diesem Buch genannten Marken und Produktnamen unterliegen warenzeichen-, marken- oder patentrechtlichem Schutz bzw. sind Warenzeichen oder eingetragene Warenzeichen der jeweiligen Inhaber. Die Wiedergabe von Marken, Produktnamen, Gebrauchsnamen, Handelsnamen, Warenbezeichnungen u.s.w. in diesem Werk berechtigt auch ohne besondere Kennzeichnung nicht zu der Annahme, dass solche Namen im Sinne der Warenzeichen- und Markenschutzgesetzgebung als frei zu betrachten wären und daher von jedermann benutzt werden dürften.

Coverbild: www.ingimage.com

Verlag: LAP LAMBERT Academic Publishing GmbH & Co. KG
Dudweiler Landstr. 99, 66123 Saarbrücken, Deutschland
Telefon +49 681 3720-310, Telefax +49 681 3720-3109
Email: info@lap-publishing.com

Herstellung in Deutschland:
Schaltungsdienst Lange o.H.G., Berlin
Books on Demand GmbH, Norderstedt
Reha GmbH, Saarbrücken
Amazon Distribution GmbH, Leipzig
ISBN: 978-3-8433-7650-1

Imprint (only for USA, GB)

Bibliographic information published by the Deutsche Nationalbibliothek: The Deutsche Nationalbibliothek lists this publication in the Deutsche Nationalbibliografie; detailed bibliographic data are available in the Internet at http://dnb.d-nb.de.

Any brand names and product names mentioned in this book are subject to trademark, brand or patent protection and are trademarks or registered trademarks of their respective holders. The use of brand names, product names, common names, trade names, product descriptions etc. even without a particular marking in this works is in no way to be construed to mean that such names may be regarded as unrestricted in respect of trademark and brand protection legislation and could thus be used by anyone.

Cover image: www.ingimage.com

Publisher: LAP LAMBERT Academic Publishing GmbH & Co. KG
Dudweiler Landstr. 99, 66123 Saarbrücken, Germany
Phone +49 681 3720-310, Fax +49 681 3720-3109
Email: info@lap-publishing.com

Printed in the U.S.A.
Printed in the U.K. by (see last page)
ISBN: 978-3-8433-7650-1

Acknowledgements

I am grateful to the Director of Collegiate Education, Chennai for having graciously permitted me to pursue this research study.

My research supervisor, Dr. V. Sumathy, Reader, Department of English, Government Arts College (Autonomous), Coimbatore, has been a source of ingenious ideas for my work. I used to lose my perspective whenever I had to handle lengthy texts. She helped me by putting the perspective back in my view through her gentle and patient guidance. Words are inadequate to express my gratitude for the quantum of efforts she took when she went about the task of correcting, organizing and editing my thesis. Her stature as a careful and impeccable teacher enthused me greatly. I shall always cherish her warmth as a friend, though she fulfilled her other two roles as philosopher and guide with equal justice.

The constant support of Mr. M. Karuna Moorthi, Head of the Department of English, Government Arts College (Autonomous), Coimbatore, and the goodwill exuded by the faculty in the Department of English need a special mention. I would like to record my sincere thanks to all of them.

The continuous encouragement of Dr. A. Mary Lily Pushpam, Principal-in-charge, Government College of Education for Women, Coimbatore provided the impetus to complete this research work in time. I also would like to thank all my friends and colleagues for all their love and support.

The staff of the libraries of SCILET, American College, Madurai, University of Madras and CDN Library, Dwanyalokha, Mysore and the Departmental library of the Department of

English, Government Arts College, Coimbatore, were kind enough to extend all possible help. I thank them very much.

I thank Dr. Jebakani Selvaraj, my friend and mentor, for her encouragement and concern. I thank my cousin Venkatesan Ramanujam who was ready to lend a helping hand by procuring and sending all the required books of Nadine Gordimer. My heartfelt thanks go to my student Dr. Joby John who readily arranged for the required books to be sent from the US. I wish to recall with gratitude all the sacrifices made by my parents for my sake. I thank my husband and daughter for having been patient all these four years as a lot of quality time was spent away from them.

Table of Contents

Shortened Titles

Burger	Burger's Daughter
Conser.	The Conservationist
Guest	A Guest of Honour
House	The House Gun
July	July's People
"Jump"	"Jump" and Other Stories
Son	My Son's Story
None	None to Accompany Me
Pickup	The Pickup
Six	Six Feet of the Country
Sport	A Sport of Nature
World	A World of Strangers

Chapter - I

Introduction

English literature studies have undergone a sea change with the democratization of English literature. English literature is no longer the monopoly of the British. With the flattening of the fortress of imperialism, much of the most exciting creative writing in English in the recent decades originates in the Commonwealth nations, which continue to have ambassadorial, cultural and linguistic ties with Britain. Many Nobel Prize winning authors like Derek Walcott, Wole Soyinka, Nadine Gordimer and a host of other Booker Prize winners like Salman Rushdie, Arundati Roy and Kiran Desai are from former colonies. In spite of arriving late on the literary scene, their works have revolutionized the traditional English literary studies.

Literary criticism today is grounded in the real world. Divorcing literary criticism and theory from either the current or the old political and cultural questions is no longer in vogue. Significant modern theories like Marxist literary theory, New Historicism, cultural materialism, feminist criticism, ecocriticism and intertextuality integrate literature with reality. Postcolonialism is no exception. According to postcolonial studies, literary texts cohere with the very political and cultural contexts in which they originate. No text can escape from the current political influence or any political theory. Writers are either conformist or non-conformist as far as the political climate is concerned. State intrusion often results in creative individuals either following or resisting the system.

5

Human history has witnessed resistance to authoritarian ways. The twenty-first century continues to witness two kinds of phenomena. The first phenomenon is the still-continuing occurrence of discrimination, though, in less perceptible forms. The trend of oppressing, and harassing people belonging to different racial groups continues to this day even after the colonizing days are over. Newspapers do report xenophobic encounters in the economically most advanced countries, not to mention the developing or underdeveloped countries. The second phenomenon is that of reconciliation or soothing of the frayed nerves of the hitherto oppressed ethnic groups by the contrition of the former colonizers.

To corroborate the first kind of occurrence, one can cite reports about neo-Nazis in Germany making threatening overtures. Racism has not completely vanished from the United States of America as well. Barack Obama, then the coloured candidate for the American presidential race, made a memorable speech in March 2008 detailing the hardships endured by blacks. Obama has held that the past colonial policy of the Americans is responsible for the present divide between blacks and whites in all occupations.

> Segregated schools were, and are, inferior schools; we still haven't fixed
> them, fifty years after Brown v. Board of Education, and the inferior education
> they provided, then and now, helps explain the pervasive achievement gap
> between today's black and white children. Legalized discrimination–where
> blacks were prevented, often through violence, from owning property. Or loans
> were not granted to African-American business-owners, or black homeowners
> could not access FHA mortgages, or blacks were excluded from unions, or
> the police force, or fire departments–meant that black families could not
> amass any meaningful wealth to bequeath to future generations. (5)

6

Obama deduces that the discriminatory politics in the past helps explain the wealth and income gap between blacks and whites, and the concentrated pockets of poverty that persist in so many of today's urban and rural communities.

Both the perpetrators and the victims do not easily forget the past. The atmosphere of violence, hunger and neglect continues to haunt them. The repercussions of repression are felt in the inferior economic and social life of the colonized. The past blunders are telling upon the present generations. Obama further states: "The legacy of defeat was passed on to future generations–those young men and increasingly young women who we see standing on street corners or languishing in our prisons, without hope or prospects for the future" (5). He also says that even for those blacks who have been successful in their lives, questions of race, and racism, continue to define their worldview in fundamental ways. Obama appreciates their feelings of hurt: "For the men and women of Reverend Wright's generation, the memories of humiliation and doubt and fear have not gone away; nor has the anger and the bitterness of those years" (5).

According to Obama, the anger of the oppressed may not be expressed in public or in front of white friends. Yet, it does find voice in the barbershop or around the kitchen table. "But the anger is real; it is powerful; and to simply wish it away, to condemn it without understanding its roots, only serves to widen the chasm of misunderstanding that exists between the races"(5).

The second occurrence has something to do with the ex-colonizers' understanding of the anger of the colonized. It involves the act of apology for the past misdeeds. Pacifying the affected races is a welcome transformation in the postcolonial world. It is done in the spirit of atonement for the past wrongs committed by the white governments in the name of development. For example, immediately after coming to power, Nelson Mandela's government set up the Truth and Reconciliation Commission to provide an opportunity for the colonizers to atone for their past sins.

An instance of the colonialists' expiation for their past wrongs happened in the year 2008. The Australian Prime Minister Kevin Rudd delivered a speech called "Apology to Australia's Indigenous Peoples" on February 13, 2008 in the Parliamentary House, Canberra. The Aborigines of Australia, the oldest continuing cultures in human history, underwent a lot of hardships and ill-treatment in the hands of their Imperial rulers. Kevin Rudd said, "We reflect in particular on the mistreatment of those who were the Stolen Generations– this blemished chapter in our nation's history. The time has come for the nation to turn a new page in Australia's history by righting the wrongs of the past and so moving forward with confidence to the future"(1).

In an attempt to pacify the natives, Kevin Rudd did the unexpected by apologizing to the aborigines on behalf of the whites' ancestors:

> We apologize for the laws and policies of successive parliaments and governments that have inflicted profound grief, suffering and loss on these our fellow Australians. We apologize especially for the removal of Aboriginal and Torres Strait Islander children from their families, their communities and their country. For the pain, suffering and hurt of these Stolen Generations, their descendents and for their families left behind, we say sorry. To the

mothers and the fathers, the brothers and the sisters, for the breaking up

families and communities, we say sorry. And for the indignity and degradation

thus inflicted on a proud people and a proud culture, we say sorry. (1)

The descendents of the affected Aborigines have welcomed Kevin Rudd's apology.

Alongside these positive developments, the postcolonial nations also witness

practices cleaving the society. There are reports that some segments in South Africa are

apprehensive about immigrants grabbing the prize occupations leaving little opportunity

for the natives. Sean Jacobs reported in The Hindu dated 21 May 2008 that at least twenty-two

people had been murdered in orchestrated attacks by groups of South Africans against

immigrants in poor townships around Johannesburg in the recent months. "Exclusive research

by the Southern African Migration Project has shown that South Africa, Botswana and

Namibia are among the most xenophobic countries in the world" (13). Asians, especially

Muslim Asians, have become targets of attack in the West.

Another report in The Hindu dated 21 April 2008 says that a twenty-one year old

year old Silicon Valley American attacked a Sikh car driver and called him an "Iraqi terrorist."

"The American was awarded nine months in jail for the hate crime after the victim told

the court he had forgiven him" (9). Hate crimes have become the order of the day.

Colonialism and postcolonialism are not bound by temporal and spatial factors, as

these examples show. Colonialism has ended, yet the residue of oppression remains.

In other words, apartheid has ended, but racism continues. One may dismiss discrimination

as a barbaric instance, but it exists even in the so-called first-world countries.

Unlike the previous white governments in South Africa, Nelson Mandela's government promised that it would oppose white domination and black domination. Reconciliation and recompense were the important programmes of the new government. Barack Obama's speech also stresses the need for the spirit of tolerance with which blacks should learn to face racist remarks. Obama states that blacks, too, need to understand whites because a similar anger exists within segments of the white community. Most working-and-middle-class Americans do not feel that they have been particularly privileged by their race. "Their experience is the immigrant experience–as far as they are concerned no one's handed them anything, they've built it from scratch. They've worked hard all their lives, many times only to see their jobs slip overseas or their pension dumped after a lifetime of labour" (5).

When one narrows down one's view from the global scenario to South Africa, one finds that this country occupies a unique position as far as its political background is concerned. South Africa had been under the British imperialistic rule for many years. However, a new kind of imperialism, under the guise of apartheid, replaced the old imperialistic regime. Critics do not agree at what point South Africa became postcolonial. There are three different occasions in history when people felt they had become independent in South Africa. Dennis Walder contends that according to some, the Union of 1910 marked the country's formal release by Britain into self-governing status; but the white South Afrikaner nationalists thought of the country's departure from the Commonwealth in 1961 as a final marker of its independence, which they identified as their own independence from British influence. Walder further states that most South Africans nowadays think of the achievement of multiracial, democratic elections in 1994 as the turning point at which the colonial structures of the past were finally being dismantled.

The important races in South Africa are those of the blacks, Afrikaners, non-Afrikaner whites, Indians and coloureds. The apartheid law that had the stamp of the rulers' approval determined their attitude towards one another. Different movements and organizations were engaged in the long and arduous fight for freedom and equality. There were diverse shades of extremism and moderateness in the different freedom movements and organizations of blacks.

Writers have a role to play wherever there are oppressive governments. It is the responsibility of the intellectuals to exercise their reason and record their protest against the unjust and scheming agenda of the powerful races. Such conscientious intellectuals have been effecting meaningful changes in the world. Commitment to democratic ideals and responsible exercise of the freedom of speech has helped shape true democracies.

It is not only the oppressed masses but also the dissident voices of the white writers that have caused social and political change. White rulers were intolerant about criticism, yet commonsense and good sense prevailed in the end.

No history of apartheid in South Africa is complete without the study of the dissident voices of writers, native and the white. Their writings form a corpus on the cause of peace. Their works stirred the conscience of the guilty. Writers like Gordimer repeatedly took up the themes of exploitation and injustice and challenged the racist government. She had the courage to talk about the delusions of 'the white man's burden.' She attacked the false assumption of whites that they were born to rule and the other races were at their mercy for development.

Under the extraordinary circumstances of apartheid rule, the literary world in South Africa was faced with the challenge of dealing with the singular theme of apartheid. "Themes are narrow, characters are stereotyped, and ambiguity and contradiction are missing" (Gallagher 381). Black and white writers had to express their views about the policy of apartheid in their literary works because they lived in a compelling period in history. Therefore, the major works of both black and white writers reflect the political, economic and social circumstances that prevailed in South Africa during apartheid. Their works help the readers conjecture the kind of social relations, political happenings and economic factors that informed art and literature. Apartheid is the main theme informing South African literature. This factor enables one to analyze South African literature in terms of colonial and postcolonial periods of that nation's history.

Modern South African literature in English had its beginning in the nineteen forties. Dorothy Driver traces the history of South African literature in English in her essay, "Modern South African Literature in English: A Reader's Guide to Some Recent Critical and Bibliographic Sources." South African literature in English is said to have begun with Alan Paton's Cry, the Beloved Country (1948), Herman Charles Bosman's Mafeking Road (1947) and Gordimer's Face to Face (1949). Urban white writers inaugurated modern South African literature in English. They departed from the traditional versions of white writers.

South African writing in English drew the attention of critics only during the nineteen fifties and sixties when Guy Butler, a South African poet and critic wrote about it. Introductory critical essays followed in the nineteen sixties when writers like Peter Abrahams, Dan Jacobson,

Nadine Gordimer, Ruth Miller, Dennis Brutus and Can Themba started writing about South African Literature. Dorothy Driver is the main source for this information.

Local literary tradition did not thrive because of suppression and bans. In 1966, the Suppression of Communism Act banned all black writers from writing. People could not read their works because they could not own those books. Many writers like Lewis Nkosi and Bessie Head left for other lands. There were two kinds of literature because of the ban: "a severely curtailed local production, on the one hand, and a literature of exile on the other hand" (Driver 99).

The oppressive states usually resort to silencing of the dissident voices of writers. Banning of the dissident literature and imprisoning the critics of the establishment cannot put an end to their voices. History has repeatedly proved this fact. South African history is no exception. After the first democratic elections in 1994, South Africa has once again opened her doors for international trade and commerce. There is a hope that the reading population in South Africa will increase gradually.

In another sense, too, South African writers have been liberated. Both writers and critics have entered a new stage. They are now free to choose themes other than apartheid related ones. In the past, they had all been preoccupied with portraying the political scenario rather than the innermost recesses of the human mind or the intricacies of human relationships. Now, the South African writers are "freed from the need merely to provide political documentation–to 'bear witness'–and also more open to the private spaces of the mind than was possible previously" (Driver 101).

During the apartheid years, the South African government allotted minimal financial support to art and literature. Most South African writers published their books in Britain and later distributed them in Africa. Bans and censorship marked cultural and literary life. Even important books written by foreign writers were banned, as there was fear that these books could cause trouble. Examples of such books were Lawrence Stone's History of the Family and Frantz Fanon's The Wretched of the Earth. There was also another queer trend. Dorothy Driver says:

> Censorship continued through the 1980s, along with an increasingly vicious political repression, although a set of deft manoeuvres on the part of the censorship authorities made it appear as if South Africans were in fact gaining access to greater intellectual freedom: the censors continued to ban "populist" writing said to be designed to provoke racial hatred or to lead to social unrest, but permitted oppositional texts unlikely to have mass appeal. (100)

Gordimer's fiction belonged to the second type. Therefore, her major works were available although several of them were temporarily banned. The ban on Gordimer's works is enough to prove that she contributed to mobilizing world opinion against apartheid. The bans gave her immense satisfaction later in life. According to The Hindu, Gordimer said, during her visit to Mumbai in November 2008, "Looking back it would be an insult if they hadn't been banned" (2).

This research analysis focuses on Gordimer's contribution to the resolution of her country's struggle to get rid of apartheid. She has expressed her concern for humanity in the fetters of legalized atrocities. She was instrumental in bringing about political and social changes by not stooping to knowledge that radiated from the centre. She dreamt of fostering human values in a divisive society. She had hope for humans living substandard lives. She comprehended the global human predicament and grasped the volatility of change.

Gordimer, now an octogenarian, was born and raised in a segregated town outside Johannesburg. Her mother was British and her father was a Jew. Gordimer began writing early. She has published fourteen novels, eighteen short-story collections, and a number of non-fiction writings. She has won countless literary awards including the Booker Prize and the Nobel Prize. She has been awarded honorary doctor-of-literature awards by more than fifteen world universities. An ardent supporter of the African National Congress and herself a political activist, she never thought of leaving the country in the face of trying circumstances. Instead, she chose to wield the weapon of fiction to expose the evils of slavery, racism and colonialism in South Africa. Gordimer had to speak for the black writers who were facing legal battles and bans. She continued to write under the extraordinary circumstances that forced other writers either to soften their approach or to shift to other friendly countries. Having absorbed the social and political texts or contexts, she embedded them in her fiction. Her fictional depiction of the real context rallied the most wanted world opinion against the apartheid government.

More than the work of any other writer, the novels of Gordimer have given imaginative and moral character to the recent history of South Africa. Starting with the publication of her book, The Lying Days (1953), she has graphed the changing patterns of response and resistance to apartheid. She has also examined the place of whites in Africa. She has hit the nail on the head with her selection of representative themes and governing motifs for novels and short stories, and her gradual shift in ideological loyalty from the liberal to the radical position. One thing that has not changed from the beginning of her

writing career has been her consistent opposition to apartheid. It was in recognition of this achievement, of having borne unrelenting and lucid narrative witness, that Gordimer was awarded the 1991 Nobel Prize for Literature.

Any meaningful literature springs from a rich cultural tradition. There was very little to recognize as a tradition as South Africa was a country with oppressive political history and strict censorship. Politics seeped into life at all levels. Even if freedom of expression was guaranteed, there was no identity for the native African writers. As a South African white writer, Gordimer was aware of working within certain constraints. Writers like her had the burden of the colonial past. This cultural vacuum or blankness was the result of the superimposition of European tradition on South African culture. Gordimer followed the European tradition and won the much-needed recognition of her Western publishers, though her stories were rooted in South Africa. A white writer who was alienated from the rest of the community by its colour and alien culture could not have reproduced the dialogue of the Afrikaners, blacks, coloureds and Indians who were occupying different social and political strata. Apartheid kept them apart in their respective grooves. Gordimer belonged to the group of English-speaking whites who had made Africa their home. She wrote with total commitment about world politics. She never lacked the courage to rise against authoritarianism though it happened to emanate from her own camp.

Politics filters through almost all of Gordimer's fiction. She could not write as if the political did not exist. Lorraine Liscio says that Gordimer is "the daughter of Austen and the female tradition whose fine observation of manners and the private life informs their portrayals of the fabric of the society" (247). It is undeniably true that both writers have been shaped by circumstances. Though Gordimer would have proceeded along the lines of Austen, the growing turmoil in her home country made her move more and more toward the political arena in her later novels. Though the personal is important for a writer, South Africa compelled her to write about the political because the political completely invaded the personal. For example, the law forbade a white tenant to bring his/her black friends home. The role of writers during the final years of the apartheid era and ensuing transition to democracy is remarkable. South African literature became important throughout the world. Writers acted in response to the widespread political turmoil and its daily effects on the people of that country. They registered their protest against state-sponsored racism.

After installing democracy in 1994, writers started contemplating measures for reconciliation and rebuilding. Gordimer is one of such contributors to nation building and national unity. Her writings raised the issues that eluded a new national identity for South Africa. She has contributed to apartheid and post-apartheid literatures that have become political narratives initiating a closer look at the merger of writing and moral values. This fact shows that there is no opposition between activists and intellectuals. Irene Wettenhall places Gordimer as a Commonwealth and English writer. She writes, "Gordimer falls into the category of writers of British descent who have grown up in a post-colonial country and whose work is studied as both English literature and Commonwealth literature" (36). She also adds that she can be grouped with Olive Schreiner and Doris Lessing, and her work bears fruitful comparison with their writing.

There is no doubt that only a black can best describe the experience of blacks. Whenever the Westerner writes about the native life, the question of authenticity arises. How accurate is the non-native in his/her portrayal of native life? The white imperialists' representation of the native life is often cliché-ridden. The imperialist writer is unable to erase the image of backwardness that is very often associated with native life. Natives resent the one-dimensional and caricaturist depiction of their poverty, cruelty and squalor in the writings of white authors.

The majority of Gordimer's fiction is not about blacks. Many of her protagonists are whites. However, her works show that she fixes the accountability on whites while depicting the squalor of the native life. She does not support the imperial mindset, nor does she have a blinkered vision. She concentrates on what she is familiar with–the white man's conscience. Gordimer might never have lived in a South African village. Yet, whenever her plot needed that kind of a setting, she portrayed the condition of blacks living in a village as perfectly as possible. A gifted writer like Gordimer could enter the other and provide convincing accounts of native life.

Colonialism has ended giving rise to postcolonialism. Many books have appeared on postcolonialism. Departments and institutions have been set up to study postcolonialism. Incidents of racial discrimination still haunt the world. Fear of another 'empire' is gripping the world after the invasion of Afghanistan and Iraq.

People belonging to the Oriental beliefs are looking at the West with suspicion. The big brotherly attitude of the Western powers raises the doubt whether there is a cleansing operation after the September 11, 2001 attacks. Questions of empire building have been raised again in view of globalization. 'American imperialism' seems to have taken the place of European imperialism. Noam Chomsky has been tirelessly fighting against the delusion of 'the white man's burden.' There is uncertainty regarding the lessons learnt through the consequences of the old imperialism.

The postcolonial phenomenon embraces more than half of the world. Postcolonial studies persist in order to give vent to the ire of the marginalized and afflicted groups of people. There ought to be a forum for the legitimate voices of the once colonized people and their descendents to be heard. Postcolonial studies are interdisciplinary in nature and their historicity and politicization cannot be denied.

Postcolonial studies are also important because very few countries escaped being colonies. Ashcroft, Griffiths and Tiffin write, "More than three-quarters of the people living in the world today have had their lives shaped by the experience of colonialism" (Empire 1). Only parts of Arabia, Persia, Afghanistan, Mongolia, Tibet, China, Siam and Japan had never been under the European Imperialistic rule. Even these countries have come under the cultural and linguistic influences of Europe. There is a felt need, even in these countries, to study the English language, which is a legacy of colonialism. The geographical and ideological sweep of colonialism is so wide that many research scholars have turned to postcolonial studies repeatedly. Versatility and diversity mark the postcolonial studies that span a vast geographical area.

19

Postcolonial studies focus on the oppressed
Role of white writers.

The present study concentrates on the contribution of a white writer to the cause of equal rights for blacks. Writers like Gordimer wrote extensively about economic exploitation and political repression. However, their share in the struggle is hardly ever mentioned by postcolonial institutions. Postcolonial studies focus on the voices of the oppressed alone. Voices of the whites in support of the oppressed are not considered worth hearing. In other words, white writers who have been individualistic thinkers with a deep sense of justice have not been given adequate representation in postcolonial studies.

White writers role

Gordimer was a South African white whom the apartheid laws did not affect personally. In spite of being unaffected by the apartheid laws, she was on the side of the blacks. She preferred to tread the path less travelled by and that has made all the difference. She deserves a legitimate place in the niche of postcolonial studies. Her voice is as rightfully heard as that of a black writer. Therefore, one need not confine postcolonial writings to ethnic writers alone. When black writers have accepted the colonizer's language as medium, white writers should be given their legitimate place in postcolonial studies.

If one were to confine oneself to the Oriental countries alone, postcolonial studies would become limited in perspective. There is more to postcolonial histories and cultures than the study of the geographically limited Orient. Postcolonialism cannot be reduced to mean the aftermath of European colonization. For example, South Africa had been subjected until recently to one of the most backward postcolonial measures–apartheid. Some critics even hold the view that the postcolonial period in South Africa begins after 1994. Susan Gallagher talks about the postcolonial period starting from the 1990s "signalled by the demise of apartheid, the first national democratic election, and the 1994 formation of the Government of National Unity headed by President Nelson Mandela" (377). Apartheid is seen as another form of colonization.

There had been opposition to colonialism since the institution of colonies. Opposition came from two quarters: political activists and intellectuals. Political opposition is adequately exposed by history whereas the intellectual opposition is ignored by history. Intellectuals and political activists went hand in hand to achieve liberty or equality. The study aims at highlighting the achievement of Gordimer in effecting political changes. She is an equal warrior in the sense that she, too, fought for the abolition of apartheid.

When one looks at the postcolonial condition, one includes, within one's purview, the shifting power relations between different parts of the world and between people within particular nation states. The study demands that one look at the continuance of the colonial legacy in the erstwhile colonies as well as the changing relationships between these cultures and within these cultures. In recent times, the term 'postcolonial' seems to be very much in use because one can see that colonial experience still persists in different forms as the former colonizers still wield their strategic and economic power over the developing countries.

HYPOTHESE

This researcher postulates the following hypotheses:

The study is carried out to prove that Gordimer consistently put up an ideological fight against apartheid. Gordimer comprehended the political forces operating in her society and she foresaw the outcome of the revolutionary activities. She also envisioned whites divested of their powers. The researcher aims at proving that Gordimer's South Africa, riddled

21

by apartheid laws, had the characteristics of the oppressed Orient where the Westerner tried to impose his/her ideologies.

The researcher attempts to fix the role played by Gordimer in redeeming South Africa from the racial quagmire. She represents the sympathetic whites' point of view. Gordimer differed from her fellow compatriots by effortlessly identifying with blacks. The study is also an endeavour to substantiate that Gordimer sincerely believed that, by abolishing the self and entering the mind of the other, one can nullify the effects of apartheid in one's personal life.

Another objective of this examination is to prove that the author identified the forces behind the extraordinary events taking place around her in order to arrive at certain general realities. The researcher also aims at proving that the weft and warp of her works is humanism.

The researcher observes how the author has used dialectical argument to arrive at truth. The study attempts to apply the term 'dialectics' in its different meanings. The term in its many meanings is applicable to Gordimer's fiction. She uses it as a simple rhetorical device, as a tool for self-realization of her characters, and as a truth-finding device predicting the logical consequences of opposing forces operating in her country.

The following novels have been included in the study: A World of Strangers (1958), A Guest of Honour (1970), The Conservationist (1974), Burger's Daughter (1979), July's People (1981), A Sport of Nature (1987), My Son's Story (1990), None to Accompany Me (1994), The House Gun (1998), and The Pickup (2001). Out of the fourteen novels written by the author, ten novels have been included for this study. The researcher found the selected novels to be an adequate representation of the author stylistically and thematically.

22

Cross-references have been made to Gordimer's short stories and other novels in order to ascertain her consistency in the stylistic and thematic patterns.

A survey of the major critical works on Gordimer has been done with a view to establish the fact that the present study has its own significance as it tries to explore the works of Gordimer from a postcolonial perspective. Kenneth Parker (1978) has given a detailed analysis of South African fiction in his <u>South African Novel in English</u>. Stephen Clingman in his <u>The Novels of Nadine Gordimer: History from the Inside</u> (1986) has made a historical analysis of her works. Dominic Head's <u>Nadine Gordimer</u> (1994) views her as a transitional writer between the realist and the modernist traditions. In his <u>Betrayals of the Body Politic: the Literary Commitments of Nadine Gordimer</u>, Andrew Vogel Ettin has written about the commitment of Gordimer throughout the period of political turmoil in South Africa.

In the past decade there has been a renewed fervour in the study of South African literature. Rita Barnard's <u>Apartheid and Beyond: South African Writers and the Politics of Place</u> is a perceptive and sensitive study of South African literature. Her interdisciplinary approach makes this book indispensable reading for anyone in the field of literature and politics. The book presents neat readings of Coetzee, Gordimer, Fugard, Tlali, and Mda, focusing on the close relationship between physical space, political space, and one's responsibility as revealed in their work. It also explores the way apartheid operated in its day-to-day functions as a geographical system of control, exerting its power through such spatial mechanisms as residential segregation, *bantustans*, passes, and prisons.

South Africa in the Global Imaginary, edited by Leon De Kock,Louise Bethlehem and Sonja Laden, is a collection of critical essays about culture and identity through the lens of post apartheid South Africa. These essays set up dialectic between South Africa's heterogeneous literary traditions and its position as a cultural symbol in Europe and the First World, revealing why South African culture is a matter of global interest. The essays deal with different stratifications of South African literature maintaining that its unity lies in diversity.

Peter D. McDonald's The Literature Police: Apartheid Censorship and its Cultural Consequences is one of the most scholarly and thorough examinations of censorship ever written. The book narrates the stories of apartheid South Africa's banned books. The book enables one to understand the forces helping and destroying literary production in South Africa during the apartheid years.

Louise Bethlehem's Skin Tight: Apartheid Literary Culture and its Aftermath traces the concealed narratives – of land, race, and gender. This book explores the hidden dimensions of South African literary history and the influence they prolong to exercise well into the post-apartheid period. It emphasizes the fact that major connections exist between late-apartheid and post-apartheid literary culture.

As all literary research depends on secondary research, it is important to investigate and review the previous research studies on Gordimer. Browsing through volumes of Dissertation Abstracts International (2006-2008) did not yield much information on research on particular works of Gordimer. However, searches under the topics of 'other', 'apartheid', 'postcolonialism', 'South African literature' and 'women novelists' gave an idea about the importance of postcolonial studies as an interdisciplinary research topic.

A brief account of the previous research on postcolonial topics is given below:

In the thesis titled "Enclosing Others in Cultural Representation" (2006), Huei-ju Wang has investigated the representation of racial Others in James Fennimore Cooper's The Pioneers, Herman Melville's Moby Dick and Joseph Conrad's Nostromo. The project appropriates Gayatri Spivak's critique of A Critique of Postcolonial Reason.

In the dissertation titled "Interactions of Race and Gender in Three Black Women's Texts" (2006), Mame Selbee Diouf has analyzed intersections of race and gender in the novels of Toni Morrison, Aminata Sow Fall and Zoë Wicomb. The findings suggest that these three black women writers reconstruct representatives of the black men and women in the writing about the history of slavery, colonization and apartheid. These three writers also respond to ways in which concepts in race and gender have been maneuvered to develop justifying theories for these three systems.

In the study titled, "Embodying History: Women, Representation and Resistance in Twentieth Century Southern African and Caribbean Literature" (2006), April Conley Kilinski has drawn conclusions about the similarities and differences informing the narratives of J. M. Coetzee, Erna Broadber, Tsitsi Dangarembga and Edwidge Danticaf. She has included works by men and women as well as white and minority authors to illuminate how the female body becomes a point of convergence for narratives of resistance in these postcolonial works. She argues that each author demonstrates the need to embrace a hybrid subject position in order to effect resistances.

In the dissertation titled "'But the Test of Absolutely Everything in Life is the Quality of the In-between:' Subjectivity in Eight Women Novelists" (2006), Micki M. Nyman reveals the different ways in which eight women novelists articulate consciousness. Olive Schreiner and Doris Lessing are among the four pairs of writers studied by Nyman. The investigator maintains that she wants to disturb the outdated belief that women are more concerned with materiality than the mind, situations rather than ideas, and what can be seen as opposed to what cannot.

"Insider / Outsider: A Postcolonial Negative Dialectic on Indo-American Cultural Assimilation" (2007) is the dissertation by Nikhil Thakur. This study explores the ways in which second-generation Hindu, Punjabi Indo-Americans, the children of Indian immigrants, have attempted to assimilate into the socio-cultural norms of individuals, middle-class lifestyle, Christian-influenced discourse, whiteness and hetero-patrimony. The investigator concludes that as the space of hybridity opens, postcolonial spaces are opened in which Hindu, Punjabi Indo-American is situated as a subject that uses cultural assimilation as a survival strategy but also resists cultural assimilation in an effort to create spaces of differences that cannot be subsumed by the mechanisms of cultural assimilation.

In the thesis titled "The Politics of Creation: The Short Story in South Africa and the United States" (2007), Lloren Addison Forster focuses on Blackness and shows how changes in its meanings reflect arguments about the short story as a fictional form. She calls it the "Politics of Creation," where Blackness and the short story shape the socially structured groupings designed to 'fix' categories of people and genres.

In her dissertation titled "Measuring the Rule: Education in Post-colonial Narrative" (2002), Linda MacKinley-Hay has observed how the education model which prepared British youth for imperial command assumed a more repressive face in the postcolonies. This thesis surveys a representative sample of the narratives of fifteen white and black, male and female, settler and indigenous writers who locate the colonial school as a site of contest. Schools and colleges have become places that nurture repressive tendencies.

The review of related research shows that postcolonial studies focus on the literary works of the oppressed classes. The voices of the writers belonging to the colonizing race are not given adequate representation. Another finding is that postcolonial studies are not strictly literary; they throw light on the social, political, cultural and anthropological aspects. There is a move towards a more inter-disciplinary approach in the studies.

Research has been done on the topics like the voice of the oppressed and the politics of commitment in the select novels of Gordimer. However, no in-depth and exclusive study of Gordimer's novels has been attempted so far. Rita Barnard stresses the need for a new characterization of South African literature: "Despite the fact that two South African writers have been awarded the Nobel Prize, South African literature is still in some ways an emerging field of inquiry and one that continues to require redefinition in view of the changed circumstances in the country" (4). The current study has been made in order to fill the gap in the Gordimer studies. It was decided to study her works from a postcolonial perspective as she has incorporated in her works the history of more than five decades of South African life.

The review of the research already conducted reveals that the themes of the representation of racial Others, interactions of race and gender, hybridity, and narratives of resistance are relevant to Gordimer studies, too. Nyman's conclusion about eight women novelists is applicable to Gordimer also. Like Olive Schreiner and Doris Lessing, Gordimer belongs to that group of writers who are concerned with the mind rather than materiality, ideas rather than situations and the unseen forces rather than the obvious ones.

The investigator has felt the need to study the oppositional side of Gordimer's texts. Therefore, dialectical aspects of her novels have been studied from a postcolonial perspective. Postcolonial concepts have been applied to her works to prove that she has been as much a postcolonial writer as any native writer has been or was. Style has found a place because the subject she chose to write about determined her complex style.

The novels have been studied using the method of close reading of the text. The study is text-based and is limited to the study of the themes and dialectics of opposites alive in a postcolonial situation. In order to study the novels from a postcolonial point of view, a distinct methodology has been adopted. The analytical reading method helps to delineate the various themes and subjects of the author. Some of Gordimer's women emerge as self-realizing characters when objectively analyzed. Close reading of the texts has helped in applying various postcolonial theories to her works. The novels are studied in relation to the theories of Edward Said, Frantz Fanon and Georg Lukács. Comparative and contrastive methods have also been used in the analysis of characters. Stylistic analysis has also been done to verify whether her subject dictated her style.

The thesis is divided into six chapters. The introductory chapter discusses the current global postcolonial situation and the role of South African English Literature in it. It has also examined the part played by Gordimer in alleviating the pain caused by the effects of apartheid. This chapter also reviews the related research studies in addition to spelling out the hypotheses of the study.

In the second chapter the researcher presents the political and literary situations that shaped Gordimer's writing career. The researcher analyses the identity crisis in South African literature and the effect of the crippling censorship laws. The chapter also discusses, how, in defiance of censorship, writers relentlessly fought against apartheid.

The third chapter sums up the themes with which Gordimer is constantly preoccupied. The chapter also deals with the different meanings of the term dialectics and how the concept, in its different senses, can be applied to Gordimer's fiction.

The fourth chapter describes various terms in postcolonial studies, as they are also applicable to Gordimer's works. The chapter also asserts that in spite of being a white writer Gordimer reflects the characteristics of postcolonialism in her works. She is a white representative writing about blacks' concerns.

The fifth chapter maintains that the controlled and distant tone of the writer is determined by the persistent theme of apartheid and its consequences. Further, the chapter seeks to prove that Gordimer's works may be narrow in their choice of themes and locale but her works do not lack concentration and depth. She has more than made up for the narrowness of the themes by turning the spotlight on the South African situation.

The concluding chapter sums up the outcome of the analytical study of the select novels of Gordimer. In addition, the chapter indicates certain other areas for further fruitful research.

In accordance with the plan mentioned above, the next chapter begins with a short account of the plurality of South African literature. It then focuses on the political and literary scenarios during apartheid and the suffocating censorship under which writers had to register their protest.

Chapter-II

Apartheid Writing: A Rewarding Merger between Literature and Politics

Louise Yelin associates Gordimer with the genre of the classical political novel, "a genre traditionally gendered masculine" (11). About Gordimer, Stead and Lessing, she has the following words to say: "In the genealogies they construct for themselves, they invoke as precursors such figures as Cervantes, Stendhal, Balzac, Dostoevsky, and Conrad" (5). Gordimer's work not only broadens one's idea of the political novel but also urges one to reconsider what is usually considered women's writing. Gordimer was brought up as a colonial; subsequently, she saw herself as a dissenter, part of a minority within and opposed to the principal white minority. Now that the country is no longer ruled by a white minority, she identifies herself as a South African who belongs to a nonracial nation. Her novels, set mainly in South Africa, explore the implications of this sense of belonging.

In this chapter the researcher presents the political and literary situations that shaped Gordimer's writing career. There is also a review of the different facets of South African literature that negates its homogeneity. The researcher examines the identity crisis in South African literature and the effect of the crippling censorship laws. The chapter also discusses, how, in defiance of censorship, writers relentlessly fought against apartheid by focusing on its retrograde features. While substantiating the case, the researcher draws upon the views of recent critics such as Rita Barnard, Louise Bethlehem, Leon de Kock, and Peter D. McDonald.

De Kock, in his seminal essay, "South Africa in the Global Imaginary," talks about the diverse fields in the South African literatures. Plurality of South African culture does not facilitate homogeneity in literary groupings and canons. He says that apart from geographical convenience, "literary entities require minimal convergence in the domains of origin, language, culture, history, and nationalism (contested or not) to become, in some sense, cohesive and inter-referential" (1). Heterogeneity is no longer a strange construct in a context of globalization, "but the South African case is peculiar because it remains to this day a scene of largely *unresolved* difference" (1). De Kock argues that homogeneity in literature is impossible because of the presence of "different languages, different nationalisms, and different notions of culture, history, and belonging in mutually excluding series and genealogies" (1). South African literature cannot be conceived as a single entity because of this "significant fault line" (1). This literature's unity resides more in its geography and circumstance than in interreferential field. Moments of conflict and division give the field its unique character.

De Kock mentions that "the most visible corpus of South African writing occurs in the English language. The historical reasons for this scenario originate "in the politics and power of the English missionary-colonial project in South Africa" (2). De Kock says that the early English literary forms were travelogue-writings and pastoral verses that related "tales of otherness, in which wild animals, Boers, and blacks are depicted as the marvelous and dreaded stuff of strangeness objectified in the amber of the reasoned English tongue" (3). The early black writing in English was "in derived English forms under the tutelage of missionaries" (3).

According to De Kock, the thematic centres of the later forms of South African English writing, both before and after the formal introduction of apartheid in 1948, were "increasingly explicit treatments of a land sundered at the heart by the politics of race and tortured by impossible trials of conscience" (3). In <u>The Empire Writes Back</u>, Ashcroft, Griffiths and Tiffin state this about different postcolonial literatures:

> What each of these literatures has in common beyond their special and distinctive regional characteristics is that they emerged in their present form out of the experience of colonization and asserted themselves by foregrounding the tension with the imperial power, and by emphasizing their differences from the assumptions of the imperial centre. It is this which makes them distinctively post-colonial. (2)

Apartheid operated in the literary arena, too. There were no interreferences between the different literatures. South African anthologists and writers tend to write for particular audiences who exclude some of the other groups who "must be regarded as part of the thoroughly polyglot South African scene with its eleven official languages" (2). Though writers such as Brink, Gordimer and Coetzee have been successful in the international publishing arena, the native African literature has not found favour with international publishers. Many international readers identify South African literature with writers such as Gordimer, Abrahams, Paton, Mphahlele, Fugard, Serote, Coetzee, Breytenbach, Brink, and Mda.

De Kock observes four mutually exclusive levels of stratification in South African literature. For Afrikaners, the basis for South African literature is found in the canon of Afrikaans literature which continues to be taught inside the country. De Kock finds that Afrikaans South Africans have expressed "a desire to inhabit the land in a fuller and more materialistic sense than their English-speaking counterparts" (4). Their political power ensured that their literature was well received and disseminated. Secondly, South African literature, according to white English speakers, is that which is approved "by the gaze of the Metropolitan approval" (6).

Thirdly, literature in the indigenous African languages remained obscure. "The importance of oral culture similarly was downgraded, as was an entire context of indigenous culture…" (4). The fourth category consisted of writers, both black and white, politically exiled under apartheid. They perceived South African literature as a site of struggle.

South African literature till the recent past was "deeply rooted in its coloniality" (3). It demonstrates "the variance, the strangeness, and the curiosity value of comically uncultivated people, wild animals, tragically doomed heathens, illiberal Boers, greedy prospectors…" (3). Kock justifies that this literature has been "*other to itself*" because "expressions of Self are often marked by a simultaneous setting apart from various Others" (3). The chief unifying factor of the South African literary historiography is the "history of its division" (5).

South African writers were trying to forge a new identity and, in the process, they suffered scars. These writers were quite conscious of their difference from the rest of the world. De Kock uses Breytenbach's expression to talk about the diversity: "The dialectics of 'here' and 'there' have haunted South Africans for so long now that one may justifiably talk of it (South Africa) as … a country of thoroughly interstitial identities" (8). In order to appreciate South African literature meaningfully, one needs "to understand the multiple constructions of identity in the country as a consequence of which the various literary subsystems came into existence" (8).

De Kock coined the phrase 'South Africa in the global imaginary' to capture "both the impositions, from without, of various identity-forming global discourses upon the territory and its people as well as forms of self-fashioning, from within, either in the image of a greater world 'out there' or in defiance of it" (8). In the context of South-African literature, "schisms, barriers, and misconceptions have been the rule, and even today it is highly problematic to shift from the first-person singular to the first person plural when talking South African – to move from 'I' to 'we' or 'us'" (9). Ever since the advent of colonization, South Africa's native identity has been mediated or modified by the sense of the greater world. De Kock holds that there is a yearning for "a common notion of the nation, a common language, or a common culture" (9).

While narrating the ongoing crisis of identity, De Kock uses the term 'seam' borrowed from Noel Mostert to refer to the function of South African studies "to suture the incommensurate" (11). He says that the seam is therefore the site of a joining together that also bears the mark of the suture. He theorizes that "a crisis of inscription is characterized by a paradoxical process: on the one hand the effort of suturing the incommensurate is an attempt to close the gap that defines it as incommensurate, and on the other this process unavoidably bears the mark of its own crisis, the seam" (11). The site of the South African literatures has been the point of convergence and divergence. In other words, any attempt at unity leaves traces of strains. As a result, identities showed the signs of becoming increasingly "hybrid and mixed" (13). The natives fought the oppositional idea of civilized and savage and transformed similar notions. The colonizers themselves recognized their inadequacy: they were "afflicted by the necessary partiality of their representations and by the unacknowledged but haunting sense of not being quite the universal subjects they thought they were" (13). Therefore, the national identity was in a state of constant flux. Gordimer, De Kock recounts, "frequently called upon a standard of universal decency" (19). She is one of the progressive authors who write so that South Africa will "cease being exceptional, different from the rest of the 'civilized world'" (19).

The late-apartheid period provided the much needed ground for the growth of representational literature. Poets and writers felt the need to build a new nation and to end the abuse of people by other people. Their works acted as agents of change. South African literature had followed diverse paths and ends, and now, it seemed to consolidate as a single institution by forming its own norms. Therefore, representational literature has functioned as a moral and political agency effecting changes. According to Louise Bethlehem, this emerging literature coincided with "the literature of the emergency" (Skin Tight 1). The phrase "literature of the emergency" has political connotations. "The policies of the apartheid State rendered South Africa a particularly anachronistic colonial spectacle" (1). Many critics and observers agree that apartheid is an extension of the universal colonial tendency for exploitation. "Apartheid, though inseparable from this global phenomenon, clearly represents an extreme and therefore starkly illuminating instance of the territorialization of power" (Barnard 5). Its study is relevant to the extent imperialism is relevant in today's world. "For apartheid can surely be grasped as a deliberate and anachronistic perpetuation or reinvention of the spatial and epistemological distortions of imperialism within one country's borders" (Barnard 47). In short, the South African situation presents a model of "human possibilities for repression, submission, complacence, endurance and resistance" (Toolan 76). Studying its pervasive power over the culture and lives of people as reflected in South African literature facilitates its applicability elsewhere.

Since a great many writers of the period reflected the insanity of the system, it is appropriate to give a short account of the contemporaries of Gordimer, since they all shared a common and yet unique background that characterized South Africa. Alan Paton Es'kia Mphahlele André Brink, Lewis Nkosi, Breyten Breytenbach, J.M. Coetzee, Zakes Mda, and Njabulo Ndebele are some of the renowned contemporaries of Gordimer.

Paton did plain speaking and his honest acceptance of white guilt touches a chord in every one. He reminded the white liberals about their responsibility:

> White South Africans must continually be reminded of the fact that they can expect no privileged position for their children in the future. Their great fear is that the wheel will turn full circle and that black privilege will replace white. Somehow they must be wakened to the fact that their present intransigence is the most likely cause of what they fear most. Somehow they must be made to realize that they have much more to gain than they can possibly lose by getting rid of the colour bar once and for all. It is Liberals who must bring them to their senses. (Paton 86)

Mphahlele was called "the Chronicler of Apartheid" by the New York Times on his death. The newspaper also hailed him as "the father of modern black South African writing." His Down Second Avenue, an intense account of his boyhood and early manhood, was a depiction of traditional rural life, and of violence and oppression in a black township in Pretoria. He recounted the experience of countless thousands of his fellow black South Africans. The conflict, both social and artistic, between African and Western identities became a major theme in his work.

Fugard, an Afrikaner writing in English, has charted the lives of the South Africa's dispossessed. Barnard states that Fugard's works are "rich texts for anyone interested in apartheid's geographies of power" (100). She also notes that "a backward glance at his oeuvre reveals that an interest in the politics of place – in such things as the 'links between physical and mental geography' or 'the relationships between ontological bewilderment and an insecure geographical position' – has informed his work from the very start.'"(98).

Brink used Afrikaans as a language to speak against the apartheid policy. His novel *Kennis van die aand* was the first Afrikaans book to be banned by the South African government. Brink belonged to one of those forward-looking writers who were condemned for writing in the European style.

Nkosi, one of the architects of contemporary black consciousness, explores themes of politics, relationships, and sexuality. He faced severe regulations on his writing due to the publishing norms. Much of his critical work deals with African literature and social concerns. As a playwright and short-story writer, he is also the most ingeniously experimental of the black South African writers.

Breytenbach was a white Afrikaner writer-activist who was imprisoned for seven years for high treason. He was a victim of the Prohibition of Mixed Marriages Act and the Immoralty act. Simon Lewis in his essay in the collection Global Imaginary writes that Breytenbach was treated as "the adversary within Afrikanerdom" (193). His writings represent "a tension between the desire for aesthetic sophistication and political impact" (183).

Coetzee's novels have an unassuming, yet powerful effect. Without naming South Africa, he evoked pictures of the country. Robert M. Post says, "Coetzee's narratives are inclined to be less straightforward, more ambiguous, and, at least on the surface, not to be about the South Africa of today" (67). He addressed eternal moral questions in a society where the minority was busy reaping the benefits at the cost of the disadvantaged majority. Post comments, "Coetzee's allegories help keep issues of humanity and justice alive" (77).

Mda situated, both in his fiction and in his academic writing, impoverished and marginal communities at center stage and emphasized the importance of a kind of territorial micropolitics to grassroots emancipation. "The experiences Mda recounts are neither spatially nor temporally confined, and the sites represented in his work – an urban shack settlement, a mountain village, a remote coastal hamlet, and so forth – are shown to be multidimensional and culturally porous" (Barnard 148). Mda acknowledged the obsessive and compulsive preoccupation with the theme of apartheid in an interview: "Apartheid dominated our lives; we could not write honestly without talking about it. The system was such that all you had to do was go into a township and take a slice of life to turn into a wonderful piece of theatre of the absurd. Writers could be reporters then" (Mda 1).

Ndebele, an acclaimed writer and academic of South Africa, is an authority on South African literature and culture. He is against keeping people pigeon-holed. "That was the problem with our past: there was a concerted attempt to define people, individuals and groups definitively, and that is impossible because in reality all of us have multiple dimensions" (int. with Nelson Mandela Foundation 1). He expects the modern South African to fashion a new identity leaving the past behind. In the same interview he holds that the challenge of being a South African is "to run away from uni-dimensional and definitive characterizations of ourselves. If we master that skill, we are in a sense preparing

ourselves adequately for the global world of the future, where to be a South African is to

understand South Africa within Africa and within the world."

This very short account of Gordimer's contemporaries is by no means exhaustive.
The aim is only to give an idea about the kind of material that went into South African
writings during apartheid. The common thread linking all these writers was their political
activism and an awareness of their social responsibility as creative artists.

These writers were deprived of intellectual freedom as there was a risk of their works
never seeing the light of day. They faced the handicap imposed by censorship that curtailed
their right to freedom of expression. South Africa witnessed a series of strange events
during the apartheid epoch when the literary assumed regulatory powers over the political
and the political assumed regulatory powers over the literary. The censorship law dictated
what should be written and what should be read. The government machinery turned into a
kind of literature-cum-culture police intent on maintaining purity of races. Telling the truth
was considered an offence by the state whereas a writer's obligation is to tell nothing but
truth. Many writers pursued social and political realism in their novels that were spurned
as propaganda. Bethlehem calls this "adherence to the testimonial dimension" as the
'trope-of-truth' (Skin Tight 2).

In spite of the suffocating political ambiance, writers were mulling over ways and
means of voicing their dissent. They felt the urgency that necessitated their remonstration.
The concepts of 'urgency' and 'agency', as used by Louise Bethlehem need a special
mention here. The lengthy title of Bethlehem's article, "'The Primary Need as Strong as

41

Hunger': The Rhetoric of Urgency in South African Literary Culture Under Apartheid"
suggests the important role played by writers who felt the urgency to depict reality so as
to alleviate pain and to ameliorate the plight of their people. The apartheid law enforcers
divorced the actual meaning from the signifiers. "The apartheid regime denied the just meanings of
essential terms like 'freedom', 'justice', 'civilization' or 'equality.' The apartheid state's
dislocations of signification are justly infamous ...." (Skin Tight 12). Dissident writing
made the architects of apartheid rethink about their doings. Bethlehem writes, "Following
the consolidation of the apartheid regime, such figures as Alan Paton, Athol Fugard, and
Gordimer lent their authority and global reputations to the truth-telling priorities of
literary dissidence, as did the Afrikaans writers Breyten Breytenbach and Andrè Brink" (2).
Literary commitment of such writers ensured the acceleration of the liberation process.
Though the 'engagement' and 'commitment' motives were questioned by writers on
aesthetic and ideological grounds, the utilitarian purpose of literature under pressing
circumstances far outweighs the pure artistic value of literature.

Paranoia drove the rulers to pass more scrupulous laws that silenced the voice of
dissident writers. At this juncture, it is worth considering in some detail the relationship
between Gordimer and the South African political establishment during the apartheid regime.
Writing has been "an extremely vexed occupation" (De Kock 8) in the context of South
Africa where censorship acted as the literature police of the political establishment. Peter
D. McDonald has presented in The Literature Police the meticulously researched data on
the functioning of the censors during the apartheid era. In an exclusive chapter on Gordimer,
McDonald analyses the reasons behind the bans.

Gordimer had already established herself as one of the most celebrated writers in the early 1960s when the censors decided to ban some of her novels including A World of Strangers, The Late Bourgeois World, and Burger's Daughter. McDonald writes, "These decisions were, on the face of it, just a further testament to the perversity of their literary guardianship" (219). All the novels of Gordimer, with the exception of A Guest of Honour, "have a more or less contemporary South African setting" (220). Most of her books focus on "the struggle various white protagonists … have coming to terms with themselves, their histories, and their responsibilities within the shifting politics of the resistance from the 1950s to the 1970s" (McDonald 220). All the books "reflect Gordimer's preoccupation with the interpenetration of the public world of apartheid politics and the apparently private spheres of the family, friendships, sexuality, and, indeed individual thought and feeling" (220). Politics is a character in her novels as in South Africa. "Seen in this way she was an interventionist, perhaps even a 'committed' or 'protest' novelist from the outset" (220), though Gordimer herself detested being "labelled a protest writer" (Gordimer qtd. in McDonald 220). As Gordimer's works began to include more of the political intertexts interwoven into them, critics began to question her literary status. This was also a concern of her publishers. The editors of the New Yorker had begun to reject her work because it was "becoming more political" (McDonald 221).

Since Gordimer's narrative style was marked by obscurity, some of her works escaped banning. The author's conviction in winning the rights of the natives is evident, though her choice of abstract and complex narrative style implies that the censorship laws would not brook her openly siding with the natives. McDonald notes that her level of difficulty sometimes saved her works from bans. For example, he quotes one of the censors by

43

saying that they did not think of banning <u>Burger's Daughter</u> because it would reach only "literary specialists" and those who had "a particular interest in subversive movements in South Africa" (239). People belonging to such movements would "in all likelihood be familiar with these arguments" (239).

Rita Barnard's <u>Apartheid and Beyond: South African Writers and the Politics of Place</u> is an examination of South African literature of the period between 1948 and 2000, years during which Gordimer was imaginatively very active and created some of her most influential books. Rita Barnard takes the metaphor of 'home' or 'place' at face value and examines "the way in which domestic space, especially the white suburban home, functions as an ideological apparatus for the reproduction of racial and gendered subjectivities in South Africa" (10). Barnard has used the texts of J. M. Coetzee, Gordimer, Athol Fugard, Miriam Tlali, and Zakes Mda to substantiate her notion that apartheid has had a remarkable impact on literary and cultural production. According to Barnard, their works seem to project the ideological conflict on the geographical situatedness. Their books contain "ideological and dystopian aspects of South African social space, as well as the possibilities and the emerging realities of its transformation" (Barnard 4).

Gordimer could not physically move from her white background, but she mentally left the white fortress of apartheid and identified with blacks. The stirring of her consciousness led to her siding with those living on the fringes. "Gordimer described her own political awakening as a process of first leaving her 'mother's house' and then 'leaving the house of the white race'" (Barnard 10). According to Barnard, the white suburban home was the place where racial and gender differences surfaced initially.

44

Barnard noted that "the official 'map of human relations' decreed by apartheid is, in fact, confined to the white suburban home, the very site from which it is virtually impossible to engage with 'great problems' – with the real conditions of existence in South Africa" (Barnard 48). "The house is represented in her work as the quintessential colonial space; the most intimate of South Africa's many ideological enclosures" (Barnard 48). Rita Barnard suggests that when there are sections of people starving in the vicinity of the extremely affluent, the law-makers tried to place them in a corner where they would be conveniently forgotten. Displacement and dislocation are favorite themes of writers who depicted the apartheid and post-apartheid evils. "The novel, in other words, takes on the task of bringing to consciousness what is 'round the corner' or even 'in their houses' – whatever is placed (socially and spatially) where it can conveniently be ignored" (Barnard 48).

'Role' and 'territory' merge to express social relations. In a divided society, these distinctions cannot really be drawn. Barnard writes, "'Role' and 'territory' are inextricably conflated in the daily exercise of power, a conflation that is neatly expressed in an oppressive cliche: 'One must know one's place'" (43-44). The characters are as much shaped by their 'place' and the race relations are also determined by 'place'. "Places are not just metaphorically expressive in Gordimer's work (as they almost always are in realist novels) but are also conceived of as ideologically productive: the ordinary enclosures in which we live shape, as much as they represent, dominant social relations" (Barnard 44).

The place in the literal sense and "one's own place" in the metaphorical sense are interconnected. One's literal place tells one's social place. The crux of her writings is the awareness of 'place' in the two senses. Knowing one's place in both the senses will lead to a third meaning: to know its possible "creativity for social action", according to Barnard. She also calls it "cognitive mapping" (9). Barnard says, "At the heart of each of my readings (though variously configured) is a socio- spatial dialectic – one that is most economically expressed in the phrase 'knowing one's place.'" (3) The idea of 'knowing one's place' holds a liberatory promise for Barnard: "'its witting ambiguity also implies that there is some pregnant meshing of the two meanings, and that from this meaning can arise a third meaning: to 'know one's place' can imply an appreciation of its possibilities, to know its potential creativity for social action" (4).

People need to revise their understanding of their own positions in relation to 'others'. This knowledge will enable them for social action. "Indeed, Jameson has admitted on occasion that 'cognitive mapping' might be taken as a code word for class consciousness, and it is this resonance of the term that I would like us, above all, to keep in mind" (Barnard 46).

Barnard says that all the essential political features of "South Africa's 'pigmentocratic industrialized state' were fundamentally space-dependent" (6). She explains her notion of the physical 'locale' connoting one's social and political place by quoting from July's People, The House Gun, The Conservationist and None to Accompany Me. Gordimer has explored the possibilities of new ideologies, new mappings of the self in relation to "other." New cognitive maps are drawn with fresh self-comprehension. "It is with respect to emergent social space that literature, with its capacity to rewrite and reinvent new identities, new stories, and new maps, has been and will be of particular interest" (Barnard 4). Barnard says the role of writers is to situate one in the scheme of things so that one has the proper perspective about one's intentions and motives. "It is in its emphasis on the difference that class or one's 'place in the economy' makes that the novel's critique of character, its explosion of roles and places, becomes a form of cognitive mapping"(64).

Gordimer has examined her own place as a white writer in South Africa. She felt the inadequacies of being a white, while writing about blacks. Any writer's attempt to present in South Africa a totality of human experience within his own country is subverted before he sets down the word. While talking about the conditions under which her country's literature is produced, Gordimer wrote in her essay," English-Language Literature and Politics in South Africa":

> As a white man, his fortunes may change; the one thing he cannot experience is blackness–with all that implies. As a black man, the one thing he cannot experience is whiteness–with all that implies. There is no social mobility across the colour line. The identification of class with colour means that breaching colour barrier is much more effective, from the point of view of limiting the writer's intimate knowledge of his society than any class barrier has ever been. (118)

Next, the author says that the black writer, too, is confined to the lopsided portrayal of South African life. He writes from the 'inside' about the experience of the black masses, because the colour-bar keeps him steeped in its circumstances, confined in a black township and carrying a pass that regulates his movements from the day he is born to the status of 'piccanin' to the day he is buried in a segregated cemetery. Gordimer does not acquit the white writer of his guilt and partial ignorance. She writes in the same essay, "The white writer, especially quarantined in his test-tube elite existence, is cut off by enforced privilege from the greater part of the society in which he lives" (118). He is totally unaware of the life of the proletariat, the nineteen million whose potential of experience he does not share, from the day he is born 'bass' to the day he is buried in his segregated cemetery.

Politics influenced the literary rhetoric of South Africa. The political rhetoric is inexorably intertwined with the literary expression. The lexis of political discourses of leaders like Nelson Mandela is about discrimination in terms of geographical 'place.' The political struggle was against the geographical divisions and disparity. It is no wonder that the same spatial vocabulary that marked the speeches and writings of the revolutionary leaders figured in the pages of writers. In the words of Mandela, South Africa is a land of extremes and remarkable contrasts. The following quotations from Mandela are replete with spatial images:

> Forty per cent of the Africans live in hopelessly overcrowded and, in some cases, drought-stricken Reserves, where soil erosion and overworking of the soil makes it impossible for them to live properly off the land. Thirty per cent are labourers, labour tenants, and squatters on white farms who work and live under conditions similar to those of the serfs of the Middle Ages. The other thirty per cent live in towns where they have developed economic and social habits, which bring them closer in many respects to white standards. Yet most Africans, even in this group, are impoverished by low incomes and high cost of living. (11)

In 1964, Mandela announced the purpose of the struggle, "Africans want to be allowed to live where they obtain work, and not be endorsed out of an area because they were not born there" (13). Mandela enumerates the fundamental rights that blacks crave for: "Africans want to be allowed to own land in places where they work and not to be obliged to live in rented houses, which they can never call their own. Africans want to be part of the general population, and not confined to living in their own ghettoes" (13). He further states, "African men want to have their wives and children to live with them where they work, and not be forced into an unnatural existence in men's hostels. African women want to be with their men folk and not be left permanently widowed in the Reserves" (13).

The lexis of politics and that of literature in the South African context intersect in many ways. The methods and consequences of the enforced geographical divisions and the problems of migratory labour are the recurring themes of writers. One finds the same themes overlapping in the political discourse of the country. Out of the merger of the political and the literary was born an awakening that was the beginning of the end of apartheid.

The next chapter analyses how the personal/private themes and public/political themes are ingrained in Gordimer's novels.

Chapter - III

Themes: The Labyrinth of Human Life

"Nothing I say here will be as true as my fiction"

(Gordimer. qtd. in Knipp 37).

Gordimer believes that imaginary or fictional narratives can often tell a greater truth than other forms of discourse. This chapter seeks to analyze the various themes Gordimer's imaginative novels present to the readers. She is a living legend who witnessed the apartheid drama being performed in South Africa; she is a novelist who saw apartheid being annulled; she is also an artist who is observing the post-apartheid political and social changes being enacted in her country in the twenty-first century. She has had a relatively long life span and her literary life that started in her early teens covers a stress-filled, tumultuous and extraordinary period in South African history.

Gordimer's life and her art are closely intertwined with contemporary South African life. The predominant feature of her writings is that she holds up a mirror to South African history. While doing so, she does not portray the lopsided history of South Africa; her vision is not prejudiced or blinkered. As much as history shaped her writings, her writings helped shape the history of her country. The American critic J. Hillis Miller has said, "Works of literature do not simply reflect or are not simply caused by their contexts. They have a productive effect in history . . . the publication of these works was itself a political or historical event that in some way changed history" (qtd. in Walder 190-191). Gordimer's works prove this statement true.

50

What distinguishes Gordimer from other recorders of history is her ability to find insights into facts. She witnessed the apartheid drama that revealed the opposing interests of the divided society. Robert Green feels that her power as a novelist resides in the fact that she has the "ability to comprehend the pull of unseen, yet strongly felt historical forces" (554). The apartheid experience is at the centre of her fiction with blacks' emancipatory efforts at the periphery. On the one hand, the power-hungry white government was trying to perpetuate itself, and on the other, the liberation-hungry blacks were fighting against the odds of imperialism to be equal. For Gordimer, this local conflict symbolized the general struggle between the perpetrators of all forms of colonization and the subjugated. The thesis focuses on the opposite forces about which Gordimer was concerned.

The crux of the thesis is the study of the dialectic operating in Gordimer's works. *Dialectic definition* Dialectic is a polysemous term. According to <u>Oxford Advanced Learner's Dictionary</u>, dialectic is "a method of discovering the truth of ideas by discussion and logical argument and by considering ideas that are opposed to each other." Dialectic is also a persuasive technique used to resolve the disagreement through rational discussion. In this sense, it is a tool to understand reality and the way things change. There is a dialogue of opposite forces leading to qualitative change in the direction of the dialogue.

<u>Webster's Third New International Dictionary</u> lists the different meanings of the term. Derived from Latin *dialectica* the term primarily means the theory and practice of weighing and reconciling juxtaposed and contradictory arguments for arriving at truth especially through discussion and debate. "Dialectic" can also refer to an understanding of how one can or should perceive the world, an assertion of the interconnected, contradictory

and dynamic nature of the world outside one's perception of it, or a method of presentation of ideas or conclusions.

Webster's Third New International Dictionary also includes the Marxian connotation of the word. Dialectic, in Marxist ideology, refers to "the process of self-development or unfolding (as of an action, event, idea, ideology, movement or institution) through the stages of thesis, antithesis and synthesis in accordance with the laws of dialectical materialism." It also refers to any systematic reasoning, exposition or argument especially in literature that juxtaposes opposed or contradictory ideas. A dialectical argument usually seeks to resolve the conflict.

The term 'dialectic' can be applied to Gordimer's works in more than one sense of the term. Gordimer's whole gamut of literary output can be termed as her attempt to externalize the inner conflicts of her characters in order to resolve them. In The Conservationist, the truth that Africa belongs to the natives is driven home to Mehring through a series of internal debates, which persist in spite of his attempts to bury the truth.

Conflict deepens in A Guest of Honour between the rulers and the dissidents. Colonel Bray feels compelled to take sides with the opposition to overthrow the government headed by his friend Mweta, as Mweta's government becomes increasingly intolerant of labour unions. Mweta and Shinza represent the opposing or contradictory points of view. Shinza, who was once a friend and guide to Mweta, is slowly distanced from the government headed by Mweta. Shinza feels that some of Mweta's foreign policies take the country no farther than the colonial period. Shinza keeps vigil to see that President Mweta's policies do not affect the labourers and the poor. The twist in Bray's role forms the core of the novel.

Bray who comes to this African country at the invitation of Mweta soon finds himself in the eye of the storm. The conflict is intensified by the fact that Bray was a common friend of both Mweta and Shinza in their younger years. Bray also senses that Mweta's government is incompetent in dealing with the labour problem. Bray's sympathies slowly tilt towards Shinza and he cannot refuse when Shinza seeks his help in garnering support outside the country for his anti-government movement.

Bray feels that he is incapable of inaction under these circumstances. Going against his loyalties, he tries to be steadfast in his commitment to his convictions and political beliefs, which are similar to Shinza's. The uncertain attitude or dilemma of James Bray prompts him to side with Shinza because his own convictions have affinity with Shinza's. Mweta's government is anti-proletariat; it undemocratically tries to repress the activities of labour unions. There is violence and bloodshed as a result. Under these circumstances, peace and freedom can be achieved only through foul means. Therefore, he agrees to gather support for Shinza's rebellious plans outside the country. "There would be waste and confusion. He was party to it, part of it. The means, as always, would be dubious. He had no others to offer with any hope of achieving the end, and as he accepted the necessity of the end, he had no choice" (A Guest of Honour 465).

Dialectical disagreement also figures within the family and within the party as there is between the people of the country. In A Guest of Honour, Hjalmar Wentz and his wife are examples for the ongoing debate within the family. The husband holds a liberal view, whereas the wife is a die-hard colonialist.

Dialectical opposition of two interests or two traits in a character leads to a resolution to act in a particular way. In other words, conflict within the mind of a character gives rise to self-realization. The interplay between the subjective choice and the objective reality leads the character to take a crucial decision. It is worth considering here to see what Georg Lukács says about a character's abstract and concrete potentialities in his essay, "The Ideology of Modernism." In this essay, Lukács makes the point that 'abstract potentiality' belongs wholly to the realm of subjectivity, whereas 'concrete potentiality' is concerned with the dialectic between the individual's subjectivity and the objective reality. Concrete potentiality refers to the crucial decision made by a character as the result of the interaction between the character and the environment. Overpowering the subjectivity, the self achieves its full potential.

Three of Gordimer's women characters Rosa, Aila, and Hillela achieve their concrete potentiality through their interaction with the milieu. Rosa's mind is engaged in a prolonged battle between the yearning for a personal life and the influence of her father to put the society before self. She realizes her concrete potentialities at the end of the conflict. Rosa Burger finds the solution that her happiness lies in serving humanity. Both her father's communism and her choice to serve the community are directed towards alleviating the pain of humanity. Irrespective of their ideological leanings, the father and the daughter devote their lives to serve the cause of the suffering humanity.

One finds the interaction of character and environment in the characters of Aila and Rosa also. The decision of the character or the 'concrete potentiality' emerges at a crucial phase in these individuals' development. Towards the end of the novel, Aila occupies the central position by participating in clandestine revolutionary activities.

Lukács made the distinction between surface realism and the truthful reflection of reality. According to Lukács, a character that has no contact with the world does not grow and that type of reality is static. True to Lukács' idea of a growing individual, Gordimer does not glorify her characters' subjectivity. Rather, her characters live in close proximity to the objective reality of their environment. Without a character's involvement with the environment, he or she will not achieve development. Lukács says, "For it is just the opposition between a man and his environment that determines the development of his personality. There is no great hero of fiction–from Homer's Achilles to Mann's Leverkühn or Sholokhov's Melyekov–whose personality is not the product of such an opposition" (482). Therefore, a character's self-development is the outcome of his or her interaction with the environment. There is dialectic or a conflict at the end of which there is self-realization as in the cases of Rosa and Aila.

Synthesis at the end of dialectical opposition can be a surprise. Maureen, in July's People, acts in baffled manner in the end, because her self-revelation is too much for her. There is a difference between the dialectical positions in July's People and Burger's Daughter. Maureen's conflict in the end lays bares her hypocrisy and false liberalism. She is able to see her own revealed image. The synthesis here lies in self-knowledge. Her inadequacies are exposed. Her understanding of suffering and politics is very shallow. She has had the false satisfaction of treating her servants kindly. She lacks the perception of Rosa. She could never universalize suffering and exploitation. The unpredictability of Maureen' character reveals her 'potentiality' or possibility of her behaviour. Georg Lukács says, "But in life potentiality can, of course, become reality. Situations arise in which a man is confronted with a choice; and in the act of choice a man's character may reveal itself in a light that surprises himself" (478).

This potentiality or decision to act is a surprise in several characters. Rosa Burger in spite of her desire to lead a private life finds herself following her father's footsteps. Aila, a timid woman, is a surprise to her family and the readers when her participation in the revolutionary activities is discovered. Bray is a close friend of Mweta, yet he sympathizes with Shinza when there is a crisis. Mrs. Bamjee, the protagonist of "A Chip of Glass Ruby" springs a surprise again with her underground activities in the anti-apartheid struggle.

Burger's Daughter, too, employs the rhetorical device of dialectic. Unlike in July's People, there is a successful synthesis of the thesis and antithesis. The opposing ends of the dialectic are whether to live in the limelight and lead a public life or to be a free individual pursuing one's own life. Initially, Rosa has problems of accepting her parents' way of life. Though as a young girl she had unconsciously absorbed the ideals of her father, she rebels as a young woman against having to lead a selfless life. Her lover Conrad also makes her see the other side of life–how to live unlike her father. Her association with Katya, her father's first wife, makes her see the hedonistic life for the time being.

However, these influences are short-lived. Ultimately, her commitment to her father's ideals put her on the old familiar track. Rosa has been moulded as a public person from the beginning by her circumstances that are very hard to circumvent. In the end, she has to yield to those influences. In his essay "Narrative, History and Ideology," Richard G. Martin says,

Rosa's prolonged attempt to understand herself and her society is

dramatized in an extended dialogue between the (Leninist) Marxism

which Rosa has inherited from her father and the Freudian existentialism

of Conrad, the hedonism of Katya, the liberalism of Bernard Chebalier, the

progressive conservatism of Brandt Vemuelen, the radical black

nationalism of Duma Dhladhla, and so on. (18)

The dialectic, here, is multi-pronged. All the other forces try to pull her away from her father's influences. Each of these forces is naturally cancelled when Rosa chooses the path of humanism. She understands that she has to help those who are suffering. She takes up her work as a physiotherapist helping her patients to put one foot before the other. She has evolved her own attitude towards life.

Gordimer's novels allow one to apply the term dialectic in another meaning, too. According to Webster's Third New International Dictionary, dialectic, in pre-Socratic philosophy, meant an argument by critical examination of logical consequences of antimonies. Antimony refers to opposition of one law or rule to another law or rule or contradictions within a law. Antimony also means an apparent or real opposition, a contradiction, conflict or contrast. In Aristotelianism too, dialectic is used as a method of intellectual investigation for arguing with probability over any given problem. Here, it is an art intermediate between rhetoric and strict demonstration. There is discussion and logical reasoning leading to a convincing conclusion.

In Socratic dialogues, Socrates typically argues by cross-examining someone's claims in order to draw out a contradiction among them. Gordimer uses the device to bring the liberals to their senses. The study has identified July's People as the example for the application of the dialectical method of argument. Here, the real opposition is between the practice of apartheid law and the revolution of blacks to achieve independence. In other words, colonizers and liberation fighters are at loggerheads. The author presents the argument that the logical consequence of the real opposition would be the overthrow of the white rule. In this novel, Gordimer has demonstrated the probable situation of whites being at the receiving end. By presenting a hypothetical predicament for the whites, the author demonstrates artistically and cleverly that whites have wronged blacks for a long time. Thus, Maureen is brought to a realization by this dialectical method that her liberalism is flawed.

Dialectic can be applied to Gordimer's fiction in the Hegelian sense, too. In this sense, there is a passage of thought from a thesis through an antithesis to a synthesis; this synthesis in turn becomes a thesis for further progression. This marks the development of history and the cosmos. Hegel claimed that each stage of any social or political process is the product of contradictions inherent or implicit in the preceding stage. For Hegel, the whole of history is a fantastic dialectic. Hegel's point is that contradictions are inherent in and internal to things.

A Guest of Honour states in unmistakable terms that the universe experiences perpetual change. James Bray fears that the newly elected fledgling native government is ripped by internal strife. There is violence and bloodshed because of political factions. The end of colonial rule is the best thing to happen; yet it will not be the end of evil once for all; it will be a new beginning to a set of unforeseen challenges. No conflict ends in a complete circle; the resolution of one leads to another conflict. Yet, there is progress at every stage. There is a movement from one stage to another and the movement is spiral suggesting that there is hope for humanity at every stage.

Shinza and Mweta, who represented a unified view before independence, are poles apart now. Before independence, the party had an ideal definition for independence but now the party has to make compromises because of the government's limitations enforced by circumstances. Bray sums up what Shinza and his kind expect from the government: "To keep in front of the government the original idea of what Independence should mean, to oppose all the time against the government's acceptance of what is expedient, consistent with power. The dialectic, in fact. That's what his opposition within the Party really means" (Guest 164). Dialectic means an argument leading to a solution. The dialectical argument is not circular, but spiral. One never reverts to where one started, but moves upward, towards a solution or betterment. In other words, real opposition means constructive criticism. That is what Shinza has decided to do against the government headed by his former friend Mweta.

Women's finding their true calling when faced with unique situations in life is the next important theme in Gordimer's works. As most of the plots are situated in contemporary South Africa, the national fate is entwined with that of the individual. In such predicaments, some sensitive individuals perceive their fate linked to their nation's fate. Such individuals cannot ignore the nation's call.

The three most important characters whose development or evolution is significant are Rosa, Hillela and Aila. What unites these characters is the fact that they live in the very heart of the problem of apartheid. Hillela lives in the care of her aunt who is an activist herself. Rosa's parents are both activists, and Aila is the obedient and conscientious wife of a coloured activist. There is a total transformation in Aila's character whereas Rosa's unravels the dilemma between the personal and public spheres of her life. Hillela is a scheming person who manipulates her way to achieve her dream of a country where rainbow coloured people will live.

Rosa Burger's history and her country's history are inseparable. She grows up in a household full of legal books. Discussions on arrests, bails, legal entanglements and political problems impinge her ears. Her father Lionel Burger was a doctor-turned-political activist. When the novel opens, his activist-wife is detained in prison and Rosa is standing in front of the prison door waiting to deliver some things to her mother. Her father, as usual, is helping the relatives of other arrested activists. It is always his nature to put others before his own family.

When she was a girl, either her father or her mother was in prison most of the times. Sometimes, both of them were detained. Rosa was a precocious and responsible girl as far as political matters were concerned. In the words of one of the onlookers at the prison door, Rosa "was dry-eyed and composed . . . she was an example to all of the way a detainee's family ought to behave. Already she had taken on her mother's role in the household, giving loving support to her father, who was . . . to be detained as well" (Burger's Daughter 29). The maturity with which she handles the crisis in the family is remarkable.

The family was stoically disposed to personal and political horrors. Rosa's friend Conrad thinks, "But the Lionel Burgers of this world–personal horrors and political ones are the same to you. You live through them all. On the same level. And whatever happens—no matter what happens" (<u>Burger</u> 42).

Rosa had to fit in her studies, her work and her love affairs with these twice-monthly visits to the prison. This had to go on for years or as long as her father lived, for her father had been imprisoned for life. She could not obtain her passport because she was her father's daughter; even people who associated with her had to be prepared to be suspect because of her father's involvement in politics. She had very much wanted to study law. However, she chose medicine simply because she felt that medicine was politically innocuous. Even if she had studied law, she might not have been allowed to practice, because she was Burger's daughter.

She had been conditioned from childhood to think that imprisonment was a part of grown-up life. When her parents die, Rosa is alone for the first time in her life without any responsibility. "For us—coming from that house—that was the real definition of loneliness; to live without social responsibility" (<u>Burger</u> 77).

Rosa tries to move away from her father's associates for some time. Wanting to lead a "normal" life, Rosa leaves for France where she meets her father's first wife Madame Bagnelli, also called Katya, who had earlier divorced him because his austerity was too much for her to bear.

For some time, Rosa leads a leisurely and normal life in France. She becomes a mistress to a French professor who loves her dearly. However, Rosa is unable to continue her life in that momentum. She returns to South Africa amid the Soweto riots in nineteen seventy-six. Rosa is arrested, and she is shown as taking to prison life as naturally as fish take to water. She writes to her father's first wife Katya about her not being able to see sunlight in her cell. Though the authorities arrest her as a precaution, she rises to the occasion and takes prison life as spiritedly as her father did. Thus, the novel traces her unfolding; she finds her true calling after exploring the outside world for a short period.

Even as a schoolgirl, Rosa has had the trappings of a public figure. Yet, as she grows up after her father's death, she has a desire to give up all her political leanings and to take up a normal course of life. On the other hand, she is inevitably drawn into the political vortex. She emerges as a political figure easily adapting herself to prison life.

In her decision to return to South Africa, she has removed herself far from Gordimer's first heroine Helen Shaw. Helen Shaw of The Lying Days does not feel sad when she witnesses the violence of the May Day strike. She is not touched by the sight of a black being shot. Incapable of entering public life, she leaves for Britain. Rosa's involvement in the local life and her identification with blacks in the midst of a brutal reality distinguish her from Helen Shaw.

Though Rosa's transformation is remarkable, she is not able to withstand the rigours of the ascetic and disciplined life of an activist in the beginning. Rosa also resists the severe life style of her parents for a while. Unable to bear the stressful life of her parents, she says, "Even animals have the instinct to return from suffering. The sense to run away" (Burger 73). When she is uncertain about the next course of action, she debates within herself:

> Perhaps it was an illness not to be able to live one's life the way they did (if not the way you did, Conrad) with justice defined in terms of respect for property, innocence defended in their children's privileges, love in their procreation, and care only for each other. A sickness not to be able to ignore that condition of a healthy, ordinary life: other people's suffering. (Burger 73)

The title of the novel suggests that her life is shaped by her father's example. Even personal tragedies like her father's death while still in detention do not leave her in self-pity. Her experiences have hardened her. She surfaces as truly different even in the moments of sorrow and desolation. She emerges from the crucible a steely and unsentimental activist in the mould of her parents.

The slow evolution of her character in the midst of uncertainty is proof that it is not easy to be prepared for public life. In public life, there is no scope for private life and interests of the self. Even a private event like her first menstruation takes place in front of the prison. She is the field or ground where the public and the private meet. This is a challenge she has to meet when all her classmates lead quite normal lives.

It is not easy for a person to choose the life of a freedom fighter, especially when the fighter has all the freedom and no trouble. Had her family colluded with the rulers, they would have enjoyed all the privileges belonging to other whites. The decision is hard for Rosa, naturally.

Burger's Daughter is a tribute to white leaders who had no selfish interests in fighting for the 'other'. Rosa is prepared to face any eventuality such as the arrest of both her parents, yet, she feels, "It's impossible to conquer all fear and loss by preparation. There are always sources of desolation that aren't taken into account because no one knows what they will be" (Burger 15). She is "sick of courts, sick of prisons, sick of institutions scrubbed bare for the regulation endurance of dread and pain" (Burger 70). Yet, Rosa makes the decision, under trying circumstances, to emulate her father and not to give up.

Rosa's consciousness is fully awake to the challenges of living in South Africa. Witnessing the incidents and the phenomena around her, she is able to grasp the sad conditions prevailing in South Africa. Once, she comes across a dead man on a park bench. Life goes on round the dead man. Nobody saw how he died. This indifference to the fellow man's predicament is a symbol of the Africans ignoring the sufferings of other people. People continue to live their life while others suffer. This can even be extended to mean the way the rest of the world ignores what is going on in South Africa.

Rosa's is an inward journey as well as an outward journey. Burger's Daughter is a *bildungsroman* type of novel where the main character is involved in a quest that combines the political with the personal. This journey differentiates her from other women.

Women have been traditionally relegated to the background as far as South Africa is concerned. Rosa Burger, on the other hand, comes to the foreground to explore the public sphere where she feels at home. She has to grapple with this conflict involving the private and the public realms. These are the two polarities attracting her body and mind respectively. Karen Halil says, "These polarities are challenged and their intersections explored when

Rosa takes on the traditional male quest; it is she who becomes the traveller-hero, goes abroad, enjoys sexual trysts, tells stories and explores the public world. She reclaims her body and her desire, steps out of the spaces of silence, and finds her voice" (33).

Rosa is committed to her father. As his ideology could not be separated from South Africa, her love of her father is transferred to her country. Another incident that creates her identity happens when she returns to Johannesburg from Soweto. She witnesses a black man violently whipping a donkey that cannot pull the cart. She is able to identify all types of subjugation: animals and blacks are in a similar predicament. This is one of the moments of revelation for her. She equates this incident with what is going on in South Africa: "the infinite variety and gradation of suffering, by lash, by fear, by hunger, by solitary confinement, the camps, concentration, labour and resettlement" (Burger 208). She chooses to get involved in the anti-apartheid movement rather than remain detached.

Rosa emulates her father's unassailable conviction, principles and courage. She reaches womanhood identifying with her father's character. She imbibes his bravery, vision, dignity, kindness and tolerance.

As the title A Sport of Nature suggests, Hillela is a white character who deviates from the normal. As a norm, whites either collude with the rulers or adopt a liberal attitude with regard to the problem of apartheid. Hillela is a non-conformist and a revolutionary. Being an unconventional visionary, she deduces that sexual freedom is the route to reach progress. Hillela is an unusual woman through whom the author suggests that the only way for a white to understand a black is to cross the racial border. The best way to understand the other is to love oneself in the other.

Hillela is the antithesis of her mother Ruthie. The author suggests that her mother lived in darkness whereas Hillela saw light. Ruthie wanted "passion and tragedy" in life. According to her sister Pauline, Ruthie was never aware that "passion and tragedy" were in the lives of blacks around her. She could not recognize them because she was never aware of anything outside her skin.

> She fell in love with the sleazy dockside nightclubs, the sexuality and
> humidity, the freedom of prostitutes. That's what she kept going back for.
> To wash off the Calvinism and koshering of this place. . . . I know Ruthie.
> Poor thing, she was all our colonial bourgeois illusions rolled into one; she
> thought that was Europe. Latin. She thought it was the European culture.
> And she hated South Africa–but she thought what was wrong with this
> country was that it didn't have *that*. (A Sport of Nature 47)

Hillela is made of a different material. Her exclusive outlook makes her look outside her skin and transcend the colour barrier. She meets different people and observes life. Her awareness of the significance of the political happenings shapes her into a political animal learning to converse on different topics. She gives up being a white, which the other whites will not do. From her childhood, she refused to pay attention to colour differences: "Hillela's vision arises from her refusal to pay attention to categories among people, the most attractive characteristic of her hedonistic youth" (Peck, "What's a Poor White to Do" 82).

Gordimer never had any aversion for black skin. Gordimer is a writer for whom beauty and truth are never skin-deep. In fact, she has said in an interview with Rory Carroll, "I find black men so much more beautiful than white men" (1).

66

Bray is fascinated by the black skin and the handsome features of Shinza. Blackness fascinates Hillela. She watches the head of a black man among other white heads in the sea at Tamarisk Beach. Hillela's attention is drawn towards the black head bobbing up in the water.

> As she slowly smiled, the gestures and nod became a polite greeting for the head of the black man, now among them. To eyes accustomed to the radiance above water his blackness was a blow, pure hardness against dissolving light, his head a meteorite fallen between them into the sea, or a water-smoothed head of antiquity brought up from the depths, intact; basalt blackness the concentration of time, not pigment. Even the hair— black man's kind of hair–had resisted water and remained classically in place as a seabird's feathers or the lie of a fish's scales. (Sport 140)

Hillela is a self-proclaimed reformist from a very young age. She nurses her rebellious ideas until the end. She rebels against the patriarchal order in the white society. She identifies herself with the black people because she herself feels marginalized in the male-dominated white society. Gordimer equates the position of woman in white society with that of the blacks in the African Society. Through Hillela, the author discovers connectors between racism and patriarchy. Hillela identifies herself with the blacks in their oppression and their struggle for freedom, though she cannot give up her inheritance of privilege and guilt.

Thus, the highly creative and imaginative Hillela is a sport of nature, a deviant creature. She knows her way to climb the social and political ladder. She has an alarmingly high level of survival instinct that enables her to thrive even in hostile conditions. She is manoeuvring and manipulative, yet the author seems to appreciate her ultimate success.

In this novel, South Africa is given an imaginary name 'Azania'. Whaila Kgomani is the imaginary leader of a political party. Being ambitious and unconventional, Hillela loves Whaila, a black leader and marries him only to see him being shot dead by his enemies. Her happy life is shattered by the villainy of the white government. She avenges his death by marrying another black general, Reuel. He is a powerful West African general and political leader. She plots his course of victory, as she becomes a political statesperson with the right instincts. With him, she watches the flag of Azania unfurl over "Whaila's country." Her dream comes true in the end.

Cami Hewett describes her marriage as "hybrid marital union" which will heal apartheid. She is a "transcending hybrid," according to the critic. Hewett writes that a hybrid marriage fulfils three conditions. The first condition is to see beyond and accept values outside of the conventional, capitalist, bourgeois belief structure of his or her birth. The second condition is to re-script the traditional role of the female body to create conditions for the unity between cultures, colours and races and the third is to gain an understanding of untainted charity and a willingness to serve the family of humanity.

Gordimer's archetypal protagonist fills perfectly each of their requirements. Born in Rhodesia as a white South African Jew, Hillela is a hybrid, Gordimer's model for white Africans who seek to overthrow the racial and political oppression of black people and who subsequently survive the consequences of their success. Hillela wholeheartedly embraces otherness

68

by embodying a sense of experimentation and adventure. She deftly carves a niche in the revolution for herself, as well as in its aftermath, by trusting her ever-reliable instincts. (Hewett 63-64)

Instead of being an austere activist like Burger, Hillela is a clever and calculative revolutionary. She rallies support for the black leaders by aligning with them. Whatever be her means, she is free of white guilt. Her courage is remarkable; the killing of her husband does not deter her from fighting against the apartheid law. "Grief is a rot, it belongs with the dead, but tragedy is a sign that the struggle must go on" (Guest 230). She is prepared for the new South African destiny. During her progress as an individual, her sexuality is sublimated into political ambition. She exudes confidence of a different kind and achieves success without any qualms about the ways of achieving it. She is a new breed of South African who can shape her own future and that of her country.

Embracing the other is an oft-repeated theme in Gordimer. James Bray of A Guest of Honour transcends racism and colonial mindset. Kalimo, his former servant, learns of his arrival at Gala and he again comes to serve his old master. Bray's conflict, when Kalimo submits himself to his master as of right, is obvious. Bray is guilty that Kalimo should attend on him.

> Kalimo had taken over the household as of right; Bray felt the old fear of
> wounding someone whom circumstances put in his power. It was out of
> the question that he should send Kalimo away. He belonged to Kalimo;
> Kalimo had come more than a thousand miles out of retirement in his
> village, to claim him. The thought appalled him: to cook and clean for him
> as if his were the definitive claim on Kalimo's life. (Guest 105)

69

Like Hillela, James Bray rises above class and colour barriers when he imagines that he can easily wear the clothes used by Mweta. He is very sensitive to the feelings of blacks while they are in the proximity of whites. He can sense that illiterate blacks recoil when they are physically close to the city people. When Bray and his friends give a lift to a black man standing on a road, the black man's body language suggests his embarrassment in having to sit between white men. The black man sits "among these black and white city people like hedgehog rolled into itself at a touch" (Guest 35). At once, Bray becomes conscious of his colour. "Bray, back in the country once more, again aware of his own height and size and pinkness almost like some form of aggression he wasn't responsible for, knew that the fellow was holding himself away from contact with him" (Guest 35). Though whites like Hillela and Bray are not conscious of their colour, the behaviour of blacks reminds them of their difference.

Gordimer's novels seek to find the white woman's place in the scheme of things in South Africa. In 1959, Gordimer wrote an essay entitled "Where Do Whites Fit in?" Each of her novels reveals an exploration of possible answers to that question. Her long literary career suggests that gradually Gordimer began to trust the native woman more. In A sport of Nature, the white protagonist, Hillela, marries a black revolutionary and then, after his assassination, marries another. Though Hillela is able to effect political changes through her diplomacy and tact, the title of the novel suggests that author does not entrust white women with the political revolution. Hillela is a deviation, not the norm. In My Son's Story (1990), the white activist Hannah's commitment is to her own political beliefs and her own upward mobility. Hillela's service is motivated for the most part by

70

her political and personal ambition and her sexual attraction to black men. Therefore, the author seems to suggest that most white women may not take up the struggle seriously. Even if they do, it may be for other reasons.

Native women are shown as more politically responsible persons. Sonny's seemingly submissive wife, Aila, secretly decides in his absence to take major risks for the revolutionary struggle. When Aila is arrested, the white mistress can no longer dismiss her; therefore, Hannah breaks off her affair with Sonny. In None to Accompany Me, the black activist Sibongile rises to political prominence just as her politically tainted husband is forced to fade into the background.

Hillela and Rosa are launched into politics under different circumstances. The common factor between the two is that they are both participatory women and both belong to or are brought up by families involved in politics. Hillela is the plotting kind; politics is a fertile field for such "a sport of nature." Rosa is catapulted into politics after much contemplation and experimenting. Aila, unlike the other two, is a black woman who is initially content to live in her husband's shadow. However, she prepares herself to participate in public life.

In My Son's Story Gordimer illustrates how even meek women rise to the occasion by showing such characteristics as bravery and determination. Aila, in her early years in marriage, chooses to be the silent woman who deliberately lingers in the background allowing her husband to take the centre-stage. Her final and total transformation springs as a surprise not only to the readers but also to her son and husband.

Sonny is, in fact, disillusioned in the end about his own role in the struggle. All his life he had been harbouring the illusion that he and Hannah, his white mistress, were in the struggle. Contrary to his smugness, Hannah leaves him and the country for performing greater tasks elsewhere. She is looking for greener pastures and greater opportunities for fame. Sonny is incapacitated in the end without his lover Hannah. His son Will, too, becomes a passive writer instead of an active participant. In contrast, Aila's daughter silently involves her mother in the movement. Both mother and daughter symbolize the changing roles of women. Aila proves that she is better suited to the revolutionary life than the foreigner Hannah who is not rooted in Africa. Through Aila's character, the writer suggests that the native women should take up the struggle without waiting for the foreign women. It is not wise to rely on alien supporters in the fight for their own cause. Aila is the rightful rebel who emerges as a revolutionary at the right time. She is the emancipated black woman whose silence in the beginning has actually been her preparation and incubation stage.

Aila's transformation is partly due to her husband's infidelity. She can deduce that Hannah commands Sonny's respect because of her participation in the struggle. When she discovers Sonny's infidelity, she is forced to carve a niche for herself in the public sphere. In her appearance and attitude, she emerges a different person. Aila's changed haircut and her newfound voluble talk suggest that she is no longer a silent and timid person. She does not live in her husband's shadow any more.

Aila has become an expert in keeping political matters confidential. Her son is shocked by her vocabulary: "Where does she get that kind of jargon? It's not her turn of phrase" (My Son's Story 169). She overthrows male dominance at home and surfaces as a true revolutionary putting her family behind. She shows the same kind of equanimity and stoicism as shown by the members of the Burger family.

Sonny finally thinks of her involvement in the struggle with wild surprise. He realizes that he had not understood her. He is disillusioned about an outworn perception of Aila. Sonny resents that "he knew little of the change in her life for which, he believed, he was responsible. He knew he was having difficulty in accepting Aila as comrade" (Son 257). Aila, rejected earlier by her husband in favour of a white mistress for a comrade, becomes a revolutionary in the end. Thus, the black woman has a more constructive role than being a mere homemaker. Through her characterization of Aila, Gordimer asserts that the black woman will not to be cowed down by apartheid law. Sonza says, "Aila develops her story and voice in a political odyssey that moves from silence to articulation" (112).

Sonza compares and contrasts Aila's role with that of Sonny and Hannah. Theirs is an ideology full of sound and fury signifying nothing in the end. Aila's participation is action-oriented and dynamic. "Her political maturity runs counter to that of Sonny and Hannah, whose revolutionary activities are merely propelled by an explosion of ideas and words, and, therefore, moves from noise into forced silence" (Sonza 113). However, Aila moves from silence to strong statement; hers is a spiritual journey of selfhood or self-realization. The novel is a testimony to the centralization of women in South Africa.

The novel then becomes one about women who find their voices through the course of political action. Aila and Baby move from passive domestic roles to active political ones, while the men, Sonny and Will–hampered by assumption of their power and centrality, their sexual competitiveness and their egos–are marginalized. (Singh 18-19)

Gordimer's novels have a wide spectrum of varied themes and subjects. South African history is the next theme that engrosses the reader's attention. There are, in fact, different aspects to South African history; and a writer can concentrate on these aspects from different points of view. There are as many attitudes to South African life as there are races. Gordimer's point of view has been that of a non-Afrikaner white who stood behind blacks to support their liberation. The following pages delineate the different facets of South African history as depicted in Gordimer's fiction. Apartheid laws and their consequences form the major part of her works.

The first and foremost thing about Gordimer's fiction is the almost ubiquitous phenomenon of the cruel enactment of the apartheid laws. She refers to the actual cruel laws in her fiction, though the characterization and the situations are imaginary. Unlike magical realism, in her novels the content and the form are realistic for the most part. However, some of her important works such as July's people, A Guest of Honour and A Sport of Nature are realistic in content whereas they are non-realistic in form or setting. The setting and the characters are imaginary but the essence of the situation is real.

South Africa is the pivotal point around which all her works hinge. Radha Rao characterizes the South African condition:

One cannot but agree that there are few societies comparable to South Africa, in the intensity of her historical experience. In its combination of class, racial and cultural struggles, South Africa condenses many of the major problems facing the world–oppressed masses, power-hungry politicians, punitive measures taken to keep the lowly and the under-privileged in their places, the inhumanity of man to man, and the powerlessness of the well-intentioned . . . (97)

Gordimer depicts two different worlds that are opposing each other. A World of Strangers (1958) depicts the two faces of Johannesburg. In this novel, one finds an inkling of what Gordimer is going to write about in the rest of her career. Gordimer describes life in high societies marked by expansive dinners and hunting expeditions. She also portrays the life in the dirty hovels of blacks.

There are white characters who dare to mingle with blacks and certain other whites shun blacks in their lives. This trend in South Africa figures in many of her novels that followed A World of Strangers. Starting from her early works, Gordimer paints a completely realistic picture of the traumatic effects of apartheid on individuals and families. She has examined how political commitment of individuals affected their families in My Son's Story and Burger's Daughter. In her enlightening article "Adam's Rib" Gordimer narrates how Burger's Daughter was taken from life. The novel itself was born in the moment the author was presented a pupil in front of the prison door. The questions arose in the author: "What was she thinking? What was her sense of a family obligation that chose for her to stand there among the relatives of thieves and murderers?" (29). These questions gave birth to the novel. Before publishing the novel, the writer gave its copy to the daughter of the political activist for reading. The activist's daughter gave the comment after going though the novel, "This was our life" (29). The author cherished her comment as the best response she ever had as a novelist. In "Adam's Rib" Gordimer records her comment: "No Critic's laudation could match it; no critic's damning could destroy it" (29).

This is an example of how closely the author observed life and how realistically she presented it in her works. Realism does not mean literally portraying the incidents or facts in one's life or in a nation's life. In "Adam's Rib," Gordimer says that realism is the "truth condensed" (29). She understands the truth behind certain lives. This truth emanates though certain incidents or certain words spoken by the characters. Therefore, the books written by Gordimer are not about South Africa, they are South Africa.

The oppressive South African society made the choice of the subjects narrow but intense. Marxist critics agree that there is the social dimension that is indispensable in the study of literature. "Writers can never completely escape ideology and their social background so that the social reality of the writer will always be part of the text" (Bertens 90). This tendency to write about the political reality was omnipresent in South African literary horizon because the conflict between white rulers and black subjects was like a current by which writers found themselves carried along. Therefore, the literary text and the political context are inseparable. In this connection, Lukács has said, "Achilles and Werther, Oedipus and Tom Jones, Antigone and Anna Karenina: their individual existence . . . cannot be distinguished from their social and historical environment. Their human significance, their specific individuality cannot be separated from the context in which they were created" (476).

Using her imagination, Gordimer constantly commented on the current political and social problems and criticized the South African white government for adopting the uncivilized brutal apartheid system and political tyranny. When the whole world was watching the political anachronism in South Africa with apathy, she mobilized the world opinion against apartheid. While Gordimer gave profound insights into the historical process in her country, she also helped shape that process.

Another aspect of the theme of apartheid is the pressure exerted by it on both the black and the white lives. Whites were the beneficiaries of this cruel law. However, some conscientious whites chose to be on the side of the blacks. Such humane men and women were also victims of the apartheid law because they had to suffer since they were fighting against it. Apartheid necessitated the rise of revolutionaries. Had there not been apartheid, white dissenters would not have arisen. As Gordimer could not overlook the oppressive environment in which she found herself, she wrote the literature of the victims in South Africa. Gordimer wrote the history of the victims becoming winners and she achieved this by writing the history of the marginalized South Africa.

Gordimer was concerned with those living on the margins while she herself was living in the centre. Cecil A Abraham says:

> If we consider the society from which South African writers emerge, we observe that since the European invasion of this country the society has been riddled by changing manifestations of slavery, race discrimination and colonization. It is not surprising, therefore, that the predominant subject matter of the writers of this country is taken from the many conflicts between victim and victimizer, which exist in their society . . . (59)

77

As this quotation manifests, writers, as well as the common people, were affected by the situation of apartheid. Revolutionary activists and disagreeing writers were the products of the interaction between races, genders and classes in the politically turbulent nation.

In this connection, the theme of Black Consciousness is worth considering. Whites who took up cudgels against apartheid had to face two kinds of pressure: one from their own kind and the other from the opposite race. White rulers spurned white activists as if they were disloyal to the white government that was liberal and generous to them. Blacks did not trust white activists wholeheartedly because they thought whites were enjoying the privileges due to whites and their protest was sham, not real. It was in this context that the Black Consciousness Movement arose and its basic rule was to mistrust the white leaders. Members of the Black Consciousness Movement charged these white activists of vileness and selfishness. This movement, which came into existence in the nineteen seventies, gave rise to the Soweto Uprising. The novel, Burger's Daughter, studies this question of Black Consciousness.

The novel relates the story of a young black who turns hostile to the white family that had looked after him as a child. Bassie was Rosa's childhood friend, who lived with the Burger family because his own activist-father had died in detention. When he grows up into a young black, he is steeped in the ideology of Black Consciousness. At a meeting with Rosa Burger after many years, he cannot tolerate people eulogizing the contribution of Lionel Burger. He imagines that black leaders like his own father are sidelined whereas white leaders are given greater importance. He rings up Rosa at midnight and rants about her father and other white leaders. He accuses the Burgers of showing false interest in the lives of blacks. According to him, these white leaders work either for love of money or fame. Much perturbed by his midnight accusations, Rosa vomits before going to bed. This is her physical reaction to his verbal assault. She had seen her parents' sacrifices from close quarters; she had been a witness to other white leaders' suffering because of their participation in the struggle. This is an unjust accusation coming from a black for whose rights Burger and his kind had been fighting.

Another theme of Gordimer's fiction is the division between 'public' and 'private' lives. Rosa Burger in Burger's Daughter longs for a private life but becomes an activist in the end. Even in an earlier work, A World of Strangers, Toby Hood wonders why his family is dedicated to social causes. Toby Hood's African friend Steven wants a private life beyond the life of the revolutionary. All these characters await a change pinning their hopes on a future Africa. In spite of their participation in the public sphere, they shortly contemplate on their personal life. Gordimer's novels July's People, My Son's Story, None to Accompany Me and a host of short stories deal with the predicament of an individual in the midst of the political whirlwinds. The pressure exerted by apartheid shaped the personal life of the characters. Rosa is not an individual in the eyes of her parents; she is a tool and conduit to achieve their revolutionary ends.

Burger's Daughter reveals how Lionel Burger's first wife Katya Bagnelli had felt suffocated in her marriage with Burger. Katya writes to Rosa about her father, ". . . he was a great man, and (you) yet decide there is a whole world outside what he lived for" (264).

79

No wonder Katya was separated from him. It is impossible to love Lionel without loving his ideologies. Burger's second wife and his daughter Rosa cannot leave him because they love his ideology. Both the mother and the daughter are incarcerated in prison for loving his ideals. The novel is a poignant reminder that many ideologues have followed the footsteps of their ideologue-parents. Thus, <u>Burger's Daughter</u> is an example for activists being affected by their environment.

Another theme is the impact of apartheid on the white psyche. The white man cannot sleep; his conscience will not rest. <u>The Conservationist</u> demonstrates that even non-activists are not free from the psychological and emotional influence of apartheid. For example, the character of Mehring in <u>The Conservationist</u> is not a politician; he is a businessman and farmer. In fact, he wants to distance himself from any political activities. The more he shuns the situation, the more disturbed he becomes. His character shows that in South Africa no person can isolate himself from the political situation. Even if one does not actively participate in the political happenings, one is sure to be moved in one way or the other. Robert Green says, "All relationships in South Africa are inevitably 'social rather than personal'. The very words 'personal relationship'–to explorations of which the novel as a literary genre has been committed since the eighteenth century–is deeply problematic in the world of Gordimer's fiction" (547) .

After writing eleven novels, Gordimer chooses as her favourite, her sixth, <u>The Conservationist</u>, the one that reveals most persistently the interior life of her protagonist. Her complexity springs from her psychological analysis of Mehring's character in the political context that he consciously avoids.

In The Conservationist Mehring is a white farmer keen on conserving his farm with its natural flora and fauna. He cannot stand any one disturbing the *status quo* of his farm. His assumption that he should conserve the farm is itself farcical because the real inheritors of the farm will be blacks. The opening passage of the novel clearly denotes that the land will be owned by the generation of blacks. One of the blacks will be their leader in future. Gordimer symbolically suggests this idea through a description of a clutch of pale freckled eggs in the possession of black children.

> A clutch of pale freckled eggs set out before a half-circle of children.
> Some are squatting; the one directly behind the eggs is cross-logged like a
> vendor in a market. There is pride of ownership in that grin lifted shyly to
> the farmer's gaze. The eggs are arranged like marbles, the other children
> crowd round but you can tell they are not allowed to touch unless the
> cross-legged one gives permission. (The Conservationist 9)

The farm belongs to the white man, yet he is not in total control of his farm. This idea of possession haunts him in the form of a half-buried black corpse. Though they bury the dead man, the body resurfaces again after the rains. This connotes that the body keeps resurfacing in the mind of the farmer. Until the end, Mehring has to live with the memory of the dead man. The implication is that there is no peace for the whites who try to escape the fact of apartheid. He tries to escape the political situation by not participating in it, but it invades and pervades his consciousness in a different way. He wants to conserve his farm as a sanctuary where he can retire in peace. Kelly Hewson says, "But Gordimer's unspoken point is this: in South Africa, there can be no sanctuary. Politics is not just a climate one can seek shelter from if it is intemperate. In South Africa, politics is fate" (69).

July's People, again, narrates the stress-filled life of the Smales. Their servant July provides them shelter in his village when there is a revolution against white rulers. This is a futuristic novel, yet realistic in its perception of the future. It tells of the kind of anxious life whites would have to lead, in case they should live at the mercy of the natives. The novel depicts a South Africa, where whites are unhappy because of their uneasy conscience and blacks are unhappy because they are not treated as equals.

Apartheid law directly affected those black servants working under white masters in the city. Under the apartheid law, white masters did not allow their servants to bring their families to the city. This predicament pushed the servants to the brink. For example, July's wife hardly knows the kind of life her husband leads in the city. The city is another world for her, and her husband leads another life in the city.

My Son's Story also narrates the trauma-filled life of the individuals in a family because of their involvement in the struggle. There are two groups of people in South Africa. The majority group is driven by their goals of acquiring wealth, safeguarding their interests, success and power. Having a mission in life, feeling responsible for others and being committed to the community in which they live drives a miniscule group to lead a public life. Sonny is such a man who is simply drawn into the struggle for the sake of their kind, "the coloureds." The novel charts the life and fate of Sonny's family in the grip of the struggle. Sonny, a coloured teacher along with his wife Aila, son Will and daughter Baby, leads a quiet life until he heads a peaceful protest march by a group of black schoolchildren. His involvement in the movement becomes inevitable and his family quietly accepts this. When he loses his job because of his decision to fall in line with the leaders of the movement, his family suffers the losses.

The family also puts up with his frequent absences since prison becomes his second home. During one of his tenures in prison, Hannah Plowman, a white human rights activist visits him. As a result, a strong emotional bond develops between them culminating into an extramarital affair. The family senses this development even though Will is the only witness to the affair. Sonny's daughter reacts to his gradual neglect of the family by cutting her wrist. His quiet wife Aila shocks everyone by getting herself involved in the movement. The novel helps the reader to see moments in the life of an activist filled with anxiety, betrayal and vulnerability. These characters are all human but the apartheid condition compels them to act differently.

The travails of apartheid do not end with these problems. Inter-racial love relationships often end up in tragedy. Gordimer shows how an affair between a white woman and a black man ends in failure because of the racial feeling and colour prejudice. Her two short stories "Town Lovers" and "Country Lovers" also suggest how love affairs between black girls and white men prove to be disastrous for blacks. Inequality is evident because only blacks are ill-treated and humiliated at the end of such affairs. Whites are acquitted without any punishment.

Hope is one of the positive themes of Gordimer's novels. Though most of her novels describe the hopeless struggle, negation of human aspirations and the relentless political struggle, she shows her characters to be hopeful of the future. Burger's Daughter reveals the consoling fact that in spite of the bitter struggle, there are people who are willing to continue. July's People visualizes a future in which the children of the oppressors will have a better relationship with the oppressed. A Sport of Nature also suggests that, in future, South Africa will emerge as a rainbow nation because of inter-racial marriages.

Apart from her foremost concern for the social and political problems, Gordimer's themes also include the abject conditions under which the white and the coloured live, predictions about the future of South Africa, and the drift from liberalism to radicalism. Gordimer has touched upon the lives of South Africans in more than one way. Her themes also include racism, state-sponsored terrorism, oppression, suppression, repression, exploitation, humiliation, heroism, activism, Marxism, and humanism among other things.

Another significant theme is the development of the self though experience. Gordimer believed that a person's character is not revealed by his relationship with just another character. In fact, his true self is manifest only when one analyses his relationship with all the others. Gordimer was interested in seeing the other facets of a person. She says, again, in the interview:

> To me, writing, from the very beginning, and right until this day, is a voyage of discovery. Of the mystery of life. I am one of those people who have no religious faith, I am an atheist. I believe there is only this life. But this life is so incredible. And early on I found that you think, for instance, you know people, you think you know someone. But the person who is in a different relationship with that person knows a different person. So there are all these facets. . . . (int. with Rossouw 2)

In The Pickup, the author is not preoccupied with the theme of apartheid though racial differences are very much in the minds of certain characters. The novel traces the story of a young South African woman who makes an outward journey to know herself.

Julie who migrates to an Arab country to live with her Muslim husband endures the heat, backwardness and the impenetrability of the Arab language. Abdu, who is called Ibrahim at home, does not know how Julie will understand life at his village. Water is as gold is in her country. She has to cover her head; she can go out only in the company of her husband or some other member in the family.

Both Julie and Abdu are ashamed of their respective countries but for different reasons. Abdu is resentful that his country is dirty; Julie is embarrassed about the materialism of her country. At first, Abdu feels that Julie is a silly romantic. However, when she refuses to go to the US he concludes: "No confusion. I should know that. Like me, like me, she won't go back where she belongs. Other people tell her she belongs. She looks for somewhere else" (The Pickup 262).

Julie refuses to accompany him to a developed country because she feels it is humiliating to live as a second-rate citizen. She knows the pain of seeing him return to the same new-old humiliations that await him, doing the dirty work they don't want to do for themselves.

Life in an Arab country is in sharp contrast to life in the West or in South Africa. On more than one occasion, the author refers to the independent nature of Julie. Julie does not want to get help from her mother and father who live separately. Her parents represent the rich of the Western society who have several marriages and obviously, they overlook their children's welfare when they make decision about their marriages. In contrast, Abdu's mother is deeply religious and affectionate. Julie admires her mother-in-law's spiritual bent of mind and devotion to her family.

85

Some of Gordimer's critics had felt that she would find no themes to write about once the structure of apartheid fell. Contrary to their beliefs, she wrote novels that reflected the times. She conjured up yet another convincing novel about a very new locale and a fresh theme. The Pickup, a novel by Gordimer written in 2001, is partially about an Oriental country. This novel projects an Arab country as it appears in the eyes of a South African woman.

Gordimer depicts the plight of third world countries in The Pickup. True to the stature of a legendary writer, who is alive to her environment, she shifts her focus from apartheid to the other problems. South Africa is free of apartheid; yet, other ills like poverty, drug addiction, AIDS, beggary, prostitution, and unemployment now plague the country.

In this novel, Abdu is an "illegal" foreigner in South Africa without proper papers. This illegal immigrant, who lives on the margins of the economy, hails from the Middle East. He hates his country, which has no oil, therefore, no riches. His burning ambition is to become a legal immigrant in one of the wealthy western countries. He meets Julie, the daughter of a wealthy business magnate, Nigel Summers. Abdu thinks her father's kind of people are very practical and successful and they are welcome in any part of the world. "Relocation" or legal immigration is Abdu's ambition and Abdu hopes her people may be of help in 'relocating'.

The aspiration of the third world young men to possess a visa to a western country is realistically rendered in The Pickup. Abdu hates whatever is native and yearns for things foreign. He has to cross the hurdles of bureaucracy in order to settle down in a rich country. In his review of The Pickup Coetzee says:

> No one in our times has to endure more of the insolence of office than a third-world visa petitioner. Ibrahim, however, will swallow any amount of it as long as the beacon of "Permanent Residence" continues to blink. Permanent Residence is a blessed state. Permanent residents own the world. They have only to show their magical papers and all doors open. (4)

Abdu's country is not named. The author refers to that country as "a little-known one partitioned by colonial powers on their departure, or seceded from federations cobbled together to fill vacuums of powerlessness against the regrouping of those colonial powers under acronyms that still brand-name the world for themselves" (Pickup 12). This is also a country "where you can't tell religion apart from politics, their forms of persecution from the persecution of poverty. . ." (Pickup 12).

The novel also presents the Western perception of the Orient. According to Julie and her friends, Abdu hails from a non-descript country. Nobody has heard of its universities. In that country, one cannot find a job if one does not belong to a particular religious faction or if one is unable to pay bribe to the right people. This is the perception of the Orient among the South Africans: "no work, no development, what can you grow in a desert, corrupt government, religious oppression, cross-border conflict" (Pickup 14). The friends of Julie empathize with his plight in an alien country, which rejects him: "It is terrible. Inhuman. Disgraceful" (Pickup 19). Abdu represents the illegal immigrants of wealthier nations where they are looked upon as usurpers of opportunities.

There is tension in the relationship between the Western and Oriental cultures.

The sensibilities of an Arab youth who belongs to a conservative Muslim family are

truthfully illustrated. For example, Abdu recoils when Julies exhibits overt intimacy.

Her friends are also puzzled by his attitude. They begin to wonder whether her

relationship with the Oriental prince is "getting heavy" (Pickup 36).

Cultural disparities mark the relationship between these lovers. Julie feels there is

no need to inform her parents about her decision to marry Abdu because it is her life.

Like a typical Oriental young man, Abdu feels that her parents should know about their

decision. Abdu resents thinking that she is ashamed of introducing him to her parents,

but, in truth, she is ashamed of introducing her parents to him.

The tension between the rich and the poor nations is further evident in the attitude

of the people of the older generation. For example, the owner of the garage feels it is a

shame for Julie to choose someone like Abdu. According to Julie's parents, Abdu is just

'Someone.' He is "Black–or some sort of black" (Pickup 40-41). On the contrary, Abdu

is full of admiration for Julie's father and her people. He thinks they are interesting

people because they are successful. Julie does not share his admiration for her father and

his kind; according to her, they would stamp on one another's heads to make success.

Julie denounces the materialism of the West and yearns for the spiritualism of the East.

Gordimer has a fascination for the native life. She has great admiration for some

of the native leaders. Some of Gordimer's characters show an interest in the life of the

natives. At the same time, their own society and their culture beckon them. These characters

crave for a dual identity, both in their group and in the alien group. Even in her early novels, some of the white characters show an inclination towards black life. Wettenhall says, "Many of Gordimer's characters are renegades from the upper crust of white society, and yet alien to the seething life of the Africans, which nonetheless draws them like a magnet to warm their hands at the fire"(36). This definition holds good for Toby Hood of A World of Strangers.

Toby Hood of A World of Strangers is a young British man out to live in South Africa as a publishing agent. Unlike most of the whites who visit South Africa with prejudiced and opinionated heads, Toby comes with an open mind. He says, "I want to live! I want to see people who interest and amuse me, black, white, or any colour. I want to take care of my own relationships with men and women who come into my life, and let the abstractions of race and politics go hang. I want to live!" (World 36). He has no other agenda for visiting South Africa. He has black and white friends with whom he moves with equal ease. In fact, he looks forward to the lively parties thrown by his black friends.

One day his black friend Steven visits him at his office with an Indian. Toby asks his white typist Miss McCann to send some sandwiches to his room. She does not like to greet the two men when she enters his room. His friends, too, do not greet her. Toby is irritated by the behaviour of both his typist and his friends who return her rudeness in the same coin. That afternoon, Miss McCann arrives with a young man and hands in her resignation. Toby accepts the resignation without wanting to know the reason. He feels a nervous excitement as he has silently "insulted and menaced the girl" (World 148). Toby is aware that this incident is not the first of its kind: it is a cliché. McCann's is the usual reaction of white; it is quite predictable. Toby realizes that only his exposure to racist behaviour revealed how deeply he abhorred racism.

On the face of it, I should have been bored by the whole thing. But the fact
was that, once in it, it was not boring, it was not to be experienced as a
standard social situation, because, once in it, all the unguessed-at things
that underlie one's predictable reactions leap up and take over; one cannot
take them into account before, because they can only be touched off by
certain situations–if those situations do not happen to arise around one,
one could go through one's life innocent and ignorant of their potential
existence. (World 148)

Gordimer shows that life in South Africa has awakened in Toby a new awareness
without which he would have been ignorant and innocent. The new excitement is his
education. Life in South Africa educates him; he understands that the behaviour of the white
girl has sucked all normality out of the room in which he sat between two non-whites.
The anger is the result of the education of Toby who comes with an open mind and
liberal attitude. What happens in the room is the miniaturized and oft-repeated situation
prevailing in South Africa.

Though Toby allows himself to be carried away by the black ways, he is undecided
in the beginning. He feels sad that he cannot share his experiences at one place with
people in the other group. Toby is puzzled at the vast differences that exist between the
two races. Toby Hood says about his dilemma: "I succumbed completely to such moods.
This one took me on the instant, enclosing as a bubble, and I did not compare or relate it to
what had gone before; an Orpheus, I passed from one world to another–but neither was real
to me. For in each what sign was there that the other existed?" (A World of Strangers 197).

Toby finds no one among the whites to share his grief with, when his black friend Stephen dies. His friend Cecil wonders how he could eat with blacks. She tells him: "You know, I can't imagine it–I mean, a black man next to me at table, talking to me like anyone else. The idea of touching their hands" (World 261). Even in imagination she shrinks away from such an experiment. She cannot love Toby because she feels they lacked confidence in each other. "You're like a clam. I told you, I feel you watching me and keeping yourself to yourself. . . . Like an enemy" (World 261). This is the quintessential Toby. Toby is inimical to the stand taken by whites, and his sympathies are with blacks. He finds almost all whites typical in their attitude towards apartheid. He needs their company, yet, he is more at home with his black companions. This realization dawns on him at the end.

This novel written as early as 1958 confirms the maturity of the author; she could not stand the injustice in the name of apartheid. Her protagonist Toby is her own spokesperson. Toby's realization that he is not going to conspire with whites in the implementation of apartheid is similar to Gordimer's early anti-apartheid stand, which she maintained throughout her career.

Reversal of perspective is a common pattern in some of Gordimer's novels. J. Arthur Honeywell wrote in his essay, "Plot in the Modern Novel" that a type of reversal and discovery operates in certain novels. According to him, the concept of certain characters is constructed with two main aspects: a public side and a private side. The public side is apparent from the few facts that are available to the reader in the early part of the novel and a private side that emerges as the reader acquires more insight into the realities of the character and his situation.

Some of the novels reveal the private side of the characters. For example, the beginning of the novel <u>July's People</u> shows Maureen to be a liberal white woman different from other whites. As the novel progresses, the real attitude of Maureen emerges. Liberals like Maureen are hypocrites. Their outward warmth to blacks is pretentious. People like her are urbanized and are not ready to give up their privileges. Maureen had always been under the impression that she had been 'non-racist' in her treatment of her servant July. She felt that she had protected July by giving him a room of his own. She used to send gifts to his wife and she even entrusted him with the house keys. She was sometimes a shield to protect July from her husband's fury. All these are only small favours or concessions. Not all these little gestures put together amount to equality. She had never honoured him as an equal.

In fact, whites must own the collective responsibility for the dismal state of the blacks. Maureen finds herself to be a representative of the hypocrites. She is mean, in the colonial manner, to her black servant once she is stripped of her privileges. She is no longer the gentle mistress she thought she was. Her meanness surfaces when she charges him with pilfering and blackmails him by threatening to reveal his relationship with the town woman. Her life in July's village reveals that she had never really bothered about July's family and his children. The author resents that she does not even know his real name. This shows that the real black is a non-entity for the whites. By giving European first names to their servants, whites try to impose their own culture and language on the natives. This is a strategy to imprint on them an inferiority complex about their own lineage.

Maureen realizes herself in July's village. She is incapable of adjusting with the black way of life. Horrified by the unhygienic and insufficient environment, she is unable to make sacrifices. She cannot speak his language and she cannot orient herself to the black way of life. On the contrary, July was capable of sacrificing for the sake of the white family back in the city. He understood their needs and served them to their satisfaction. The servant reminds her that he is nothing more than a boy in her house. "But I'm work for you. I am your boy who work for you. There in town you are trusting your boy. I . . . your boy for fifteen years" (July's People 69).

For white liberals, a servant could only be a boy; he could never be an equal. In spite of this ground reality, the author cherishes a hope for the future. This is shown by the fact that Maureen's children Gina, Victor and Royce are entirely different in their attitude towards black life. July's daughter Nyiko and Maureen's daughter Gina become friends and their camaraderie is refreshing. Through this portrayal, the author suggests that such positive changes are possible for the next generation of blacks and whites: "Nyiko has appeared early in the doorway. Her tender curls sift sunlight; one pink-soled foot hooks round tiny black ankle as she waits for her friend Gina. The little girls smile and don't speak before the others; their friendship is too deep and secret for that" (July 156-157). If adults were as open to changes as these children are, a South Africa without colour barriers would be born. Grown-up people have to be born again and be child-like in their forgetting the past differences. Whites have to change and accept change.

The study has also identified the different sections of the society that received Gordimer's tribute. Communists sympathized with the ANC's struggle and supported it.

Gordimer immortalizes the role of communists in the anti-apartheid struggle in Burger's

Daughter. Burger's character is fashioned on Nelson Mandela's defense attorney Bram

Fischer. Burger is a communist leader whose ideals helped in the fight for the abolition of

apartheid. Though the communists had a different agenda from that of the ANC members,

they co-operated with them to see the end of apartheid.

Race does not exist for the communists. Burger treats blacks and whites alike.

The communists' main aim was to remove capitalist rulers and to replace them with a

proletariat government. Freedom is the beginning for communists, whereas it was the

ultimate goal of the ANC. Nelson Mandela spoke that "for many decades Communists

were the only political group in South Africa who were prepared to treat Africans as human

beings and their equals. . . . They were the only political group, which was prepared to work

with the Africans for the attainment of political rights and a stake in society" (9). He also

averred in that speech that though there was universal condemnation of apartheid, the

louder condemnation of apartheid came from the Communist bloc. They were more

sympathetic to the plight of Afro-Asian countries that were colonized by the Capitalist

West. Burger's Daughter reveals the writer's grasp of communist ideals. She has

glorified the part played by a communist leader in the anti-apartheid struggle.

Studying Gordimer's novels in the chronological order reveals another dimension

of the writer's development as an activist. Though Gordimer was a liberal in the beginning,

the growing violence against blacks and its repercussions on the life of whites made her

reconsider her own liberal attitude. An active liberal at first, she was later disillusioned

with their movement. She began to doubt the effectiveness of moderate tactics adopted

Writer's development as an activist.

by the liberals. She thought that without absolute political commitment, equality of the blacks would only remain a dream. Liberals were those blacks and whites who were actively involved in the struggle to abolish apartheid and to extend equal rights to non-whites within the existing parliamentary structure.

The year 1948 came as defining moment in the attitude of whites towards liberalism. Liberalism had been a fashionable cult earlier. People who had had faith in equality were hardening into radicals gradually. Later, there was a need for true radicals with absolute political commitment and the will to end apartheid. Literature also reflected this change. "Three main themes emerge from a close examination of the literature: the radicalization of genuine blacks, the distinction between public and private 'livers', and the absolute nature of the demand for political commitment" (Wettenhall 36).

Gordimer portrays in her novels the initial questioning of the efficacy of liberalism. This distinct choice of radicalism is evident in A Guest of Honour. Bray is saddened by the fact that the government is becoming fascist in putting down the trade unions. As a result, he is morally compelled to side with the opposition leader Shinza. Bray concludes that safe liberalism will be harmful in such a situation. Liberalism is equal to passiveness. This would be dangerous in the end. Therefore, Bray tells Rebecca, "You're the one who told me once that playing safe was impossible, to live one must go on and do the next thing. You proposed the paradox that playing safe is dangerous. I was very impressed" (Guest 409). Her later novels show that revolution is necessary and radicalism only will help that to happen.

Gordimer equates holding liberal views to living in the eye of the storm. "That eye that meteorologists say is safe, a ball of security rolled up in fury, that eye that was whiteness" (Sport 112). Being a white liberal is playing safe. Whiteness protected them from entering the political storm, which battered the black activists. Some whites occasionally involved themselves in revolutionary activities. For example, Hillela's aunt Pauline, "given away by wild-blown hair, put her head into the cyclone briefly. Others went out and did not come back" (Sport 112). When blacks were being punished, liberal whites sympathized with them, but from the safe position of being a white. "And even those who were humanely and morally opposed, on principle, to beatings, applications of electric shocks, disorientation by extended denial of sleep, generally took their stand from under the centre of the white eye's hypnotic gaze" (Sport 113).

The novelist's attitude towards white liberals is revealed in the novel July's People in a telling manner. According to Gordimer, liberalism is a mask that peels off when there is a crisis. Liberal whites' kindness for and camaraderie with the black people are revealed as deception. They are deceitful in their outlook and this true nature in brought out only in a reversal of situation.

Beleaguered master-servant relationship is another consequence of the apartheid culture. The rich white lived largely depending on the blacks. White women who were liberal were seemingly kind to their black servants doling out small favours and little acts of charity. However, whites never harboured any illusions about the equal status of blacks and whites. Their servants were more like machines obeying their commands. Whites were never aware of the culture of their servants. Yet, black servants learnt the etiquette of whites and fulfilled their needs. There are several short stories such as "The Moment Before the Gun Went off," "Six Feet of the Country" and "Monday is Better than Sunday" which deal with the fate of black servants in South Africa.

The theme of uncertainty and the sense of waiting for a solution to the apartheid question are evident as one reads her works. Her works do not declare the end of apartheid. However, there is the foreshadowing of what is going to happen at least in July's People, A Sport of Nature and A Guest of Honour. These novels are conjectures at what might happen. As the demands for the withdrawal of the apartheid law intensified, Gordimer began to feel that change was imminent. She has used the following quotation from Gramsci as an epigraph for July's People. "The old is dying, and the new cannot be born; in this interregnum there arises a great diversity of morbid symptoms" The ending of the novel clearly denotes with certitude that South Africa is hurtling towards revolution, though the fate of the whites is left in uncertainty. Robert Green writes, "Gordimer's fiction-characters perceive their life as in a 'state of suspension' between an intolerable present and an unimaginable future, a limbo that much of Gordimer's work has chosen to inhabit" (548).

By making the conclusion of July's People ambiguous, Gordimer reflects the mood prevailing at that time. It was a period of transition and no one was aware of which direction the political winds would blow. There was also a feeling of improbability and insecurity. The period was marked by a fear of what the future held for both blacks and whites.

The feeling of insecurity was felt at the physical as well as psychological level. Several of Gordimer's short stories and some of her novels deal with the theme of fear and mutual suspicion. "Once upon a Time" is a short story dealing with the problem of insecurity. This story reads like a fairy tale. The owner of a house in the suburb is obsessed with safety arrangement for his house. There are no riots, yet the family is afraid of possible burglaries. They go in for more and more sophisticated security devices. The ultimate security device they install is described thus:

> Placed the length of walls, it consisted of a continuous coil of stiff and shining metal serrated into jagged blades, so that there would be no way of climbing over it and no way through its tunnel without getting entangled in its fangs. There would be no way out, only a struggle getting bloodier and bloodier, a deeper and sharper locking and tearing of flesh. ("Jump" and Other Stories 29)

The fence symbolically denotes the apartheid law. The white rulers imagine that the stringent law will ensure their safety. However, the oppressive law will embroil them in more and more problems. The author suggests in this parable-like short story that the white man's preoccupation with the question of security measures is in direct proportion to the extent to which blacks live in poverty. Blacks' eternal poverty and low living standards drive them to burglary. Their poverty results in the white man's single-minded pursuit of more improved security systems.

Whites' fear of blacks is the result of their oppressive policy of discrimination. A Guest of Honour is set in an unnamed Central African country. Though the country has won independence, many white settlers remain. Mr. Deal, a super-market-owner says that blacks are not prepared for independence. He says, "Lots of hooligans and no one to give them the language they understand, any more. All they have learnt is how to thieve better. You wouldn't believe it if I told you my losses since I converted to self-service. This place just isn't ready for it–you've got to have civilized people" (Guest 284).

Whites had to live in a state of 'tension.' Sometimes the white man's tension is concrete, while at other times it is unspeakable. In the short story "Six Feet of the Country," the author speaks of the indescribable fear of the white man:

> When Johannesburg people speak of tension, they don't mean hurrying
> people in crowded streets, the struggle for money, or the general
> competitive character of city life. They mean the guns under the white
> man's pillows and the burglar bars on the white man's windows.
> They mean those strange moments on city pavements when a black man
> won't stand aside for a white man. (Six Feet of the Country 8)

Danger and violence are lurking behind life in the South African society.

The novel The House Gun starts with the sentence, "Something terrible happened" (The House Gun 3). Though The House Gun was published in 1998, four years after the abolition of apartheid, danger and disaster were looming large. The House Gun, written as late as 1998, is no longer about apartheid, yet the characters are very much alive to the memories of the past. The shadow of apartheid haunts the present. The epigraph of the book, "The crime is the punishment" aptly sums up the story. Duncan, the only son of rich white parents, commits a murder. The parents, Claudia and Harald, are intelligent and highly educated. They seek the help of a prosperous and successful black lawyer

Hamilton Motsomai who himself was a victim of apartheid. The novel expresses the fear of Harold and Claudia Lindgard. "Motsomai was all there between them and the death penalty. Not only had he come from the other side; everything had come to them from the other side, the nakedness to the final disaster; powerlessness, helplessness before the law" (House 28).

Claudia is a liberal white doctor; yet, she has doubts about the intellectual capacities of blacks. She doubts whether old prejudices will come to the surface if the lawyer is a black. Herald thinks if there is a black judge on the bench, it might help. This thought makes him feel ashamed. "His voice is dry: that he should be thinking like this. Ashamed. And why should such a calculation come to mind–a black judge inclined to think better of an accused because he had chosen a black advocate–when we are not talking here of a criminal, a murderer, appearing before him. Where does such a thought come from, for God's sake!" (House 33).

Claudia is guilty of liberal political ideas. She remembers her son's school-life. As an aside the author adds, "A liberal education–whose liberalism did not extend to admitting blacks, like Motsomai–they realized now" (House 69). Claudia now realizes that though her son was white and protected from the dangers of segregation, she had other fears. "The unease they felt came from revealed knowledge that there are dangers inherent, there in the young; dangers within existence itself. There is no segregation from them" (House 69).

Men and women in Gordimer's novels experience fear and trepidation most of the time. They live in an atmosphere of rampant violence. The Soweto Revolution, ceasefires, riots, imprisonment and harassments mark the novels Burger's Daughter, My Son's Story, July's People, The House Gun, None to Accompany me, A World of Strangers, A Guest of Honour, and A Sport of Nature.

In My Son's Story, the house of Sonny is gutted by miscreants. Murders take place in A World of Strangers, A Guest of Honour and A Sport of Nature. Arson and sabotage mark July's people. In None to Accompany Me, the protagonist Vera Stark is injured and one of her colleagues is murdered. In The Conservationist, there is a murder in the beginning and uncertainty surrounds the fate of the main character at the end of the novel.

Apartheid entailed the problem of exiles. Gordimer recounts the problems faced by exiles resettling in South Africa on the eve of the declaration of the end of apartheid. None to Accompany Me deals with the extraordinary period preceding the first non-racial election and the beginning of the majority rule in South Africa.

The poignant scenes of homelessness and the human tragedy resulting from displacement mark None to Accompany Me. Blacks are considered extra baggage to be picked up and set up somewhere else. The false logic behind this act is to separate the black people from the neighbourhood of white people. Vera Stark's Legal Foundation constantly fights for justice by identifying the loopholes in the false logic.

Oupa, an ex-prisoner, gets accommodation in the suburbs with the help of the Legal Foundation. Soon, a black couple and their two children move into his flat. When another black, workless and penniless, joins them, Oupa finds it difficult to study at night because his companion is talking all the time. Vera suggests that he should be firm and ask the fellow to move somewhere else. Oupa is unable to be firm because the man was with him on the island. The friendship and the fellow-feeling he forged in prison are so strong that he cannot be rude to his former prison inmate.

The writer also speaks about the new situation arising out of the exiles returning to South African cities. The period of exile has had a tremendous influence on their individual lives. For example, Didymus and Sibongile had taken refuge in London where their daughter Mpho was born. Mpho is a lovely teenager who does not speak her parents' language. She is dissociated from the African culture. She has spent so many years in Europe that she cannot understand life in Africa. Her parents are upset when she gets inadvertently pregnant because of her relationship with Oupa. Her mother laments that they "should never have brought her from London. She should have been left at school there. You wanted her home; 'home' here, to get pregnant at school, like every girl from a location" (None 173).

Though South Africa is their native country, Sibongile hates life at the 'location', a place where blacks live. She doesn't like Mpho growing up in a South African city. Oupa says that though she is a child, she knows so many things he himself does not know. He says that even if Oupa had no wife and children, it would be impossible to marry Mpho. He has spent his prime time in prison and, therefore, in ignorance. Mpho knows more things than he does. He says about her maturity that is beyond her age: ". . . she's such a kid, the time when I might have a girl-friend like that, I was inside. . . . But also she's seen, she knows, so many things I never have–London and Europe and so on . . . sometimes she even laughs at me, the things I don't know about" (None 175-176).

Another topic one finds in three of Gordimer's novels is homosexuality. Homosexuality was originally derogatorily used to stigmatize male and female same-sex love as deviant and abnormal. Now this term has been adopted to identify a way of life. Gordimer's novels reveal the changing attitude towards homosexuality or lesbianism. One of her early novels reflects the shock at finding a homosexual. Her second novel still is not able to come to terms with this deviant behaviour. Her last work on this theme views the subject in a matter-of-fact manner.

The Conservationist is one of the earliest novels in which she uses the theme of homosexuality as a symbol of unproductive and barren future waiting for the whites in South Africa. Mehring is taking efforts to conserve the forest: his fear is that soon nothing will be left. Thus, as a father and a farmer, he is concerned about the future, whereas he finds his son Terry inclined towards homosexuality. He fears that homosexuality will not result in a future generation that will take care of the farm. Terry represents the new generation white curious to know other possibilities including homosexuality.

None to Accompany Me mentions the theme of lesbianism. Vera Stark's daughter Anne chooses to live with a woman. Vera shudders at her daughter's choice. She is proud of the fact that she could make love only to men. The author feels that this is the generation's way of enjoying the sexual freedom. When Vera was young, marriage was the only way if one wanted sex. The author concludes that the present generation has the sexual freedom and the corollary is AIDS. There is a discussion on homosexuality. "Maybe the 'cause'– can you call it that, gays themselves are furious if you suggest it's an abnormality–maybe it's physical. May be psychological. There are many theories. But Annie would say:

choice. Free choice" (None 73). Vera likens such love to a headless torso. Annie took her sculptor-father's headless torsos with her to the house where she and another woman make a home for a black child. These headless torsos represent for her the desire between woman and woman.

The third novel to include the theme of homosexuality is The House Gun. Duncan kills his ex-lover, Carl Jesperson when he finds him with his girl friend on a sofa. He is so enraged by the callous manner in which Carl dismisses the whole matter the next day. He shoots him with the gun that is readily available on the table near him. His mother who is a doctor does not at all take his homosexuality seriously. She imagines that he could have experimented at school. "In boys' schools, it's difficult to resist. But I would have thought–certainly we thought!–at a school like this, first sex would be with girls? There were enough girls available. Sex education. Girls would have been on the pill already, then, wouldn't they?" (House 119). This novel reflects the casual and cold manner in Duncan's mother views free sex and homosexuality. This callous way of treating virginity makes one recall the degradation of moral values among the affluent. As the author has been writing over a long period, the attitudinal change of people is perceptible.

Some of Gordimer's women break the established conventions as far as their personal life is concerned. According to some of her women characters, national and social values far outweigh personal values. They cross borders as far as sexuality is concerned. For Hillela and Vera Stark loyalty and fidelity are secondary because there are more pressing social mores like the unhappy predicament of blacks. Vera considers sexual freedom as an amoral question. She commits adultery and reasons out that only Ben, her second husband, showed her that she could abandon her first husband and choose another lover. "If Ben had taught her that the possibilities of eroticism were beyond experience with one man, then this meant that the total experience of love-making did not end with him" (None 61).

Vera's rationale is that her relationship with another man concerned her alone, her sexuality, a private constant in her being, a characteristic like the colour of eyes, the shape of a nose, the nature of a personal spirit that never could belong to anyone other than the self. She did not feel culpable "for the credo she had adopted for the situation was the well-worn one that anything was permitted her, was her right, so long as no one was hurt" (None 67). Thus, personal anxiety and moral questions are relegated to the background as far as Vera is concerned. Hillela also crosses the conventional borders to experiment with life.

For Vera, life transcends sex. For her, sexual fidelity never seemed more important than political happenings. Vera's second husband Ben's whole life was defined by his love for her. According to her, he put the whole weight of his life on her. She loved him but that love has changed. His love never changes. "It hasn't been taken up into other things. Children born, friends disappearing in exile, in prison, killings around us, the death of his father in the house, the whole country changing. It hasn't moved" (None 223). She tells her son that she renews her love or shifts her love to something else. "There's been so much else, since then. Ivan, I can't live in the past" (None 223). For Vera, love and sex are only a part of life. Things that are more important were the atrocities happening around her. She is an emancipated woman who can think about more important things than sex. One cannot nail her down in a relationship or put a stamp on her relationship with any man.

Gordimer's heroine has a Lawrentian attitude towards man-woman relationship. What D. H. Lawrence said in "Morality and the Novel" about man-woman relationship holds good for Vera, too.

> As for the bond of love, better put it off when it galls. It is an absurdity, to say that men and women *must love*. Men and women will be forever subtly and changingly related to one another; no need to yoke them with any 'bond' at all. The only morality is to have man true to manhood, woman to her womanhood, and let the relationship form of itself, in all honour. For it is, to each, *life itself*. (130)

Prophetic vision is a part of Gordimer's contribution. She was endowed with creativity and foresight. Her far-sightedness is evident in The Conservationist, A Sport of Nature, July's People and A Guest of Honour. The Royal Swedish Academy complimented her richly on the realization of her prophetic vision.

In The Conservationist, Gordimer juxtaposes the barren future of whites with the African myth on creation. Mehring's ambitions of conservation are not to be realized. As the opening paragraph suggests the "pale freckled eggs" are to be possessed or owned by the future generations of blacks, not whites. Mehring's son Terry insists that the farm hands call him 'Terry' and not 'master.' He is also inclined towards homosexuality. Gordimer uses this characteristic of the son to forewarn Mehring that his son or his progeny will not inherit the farm. In contrast, in the epigraph of the novel, Gordimer quotes from Reverend Henry Callaway's <u>The Religious System of the Amazulu</u> dealing with the tradition of creation and Ancestor Worship. ". . . I ask also for children, that this village may have a large population, and your name may never come to an end" (<u>Conser</u>. 61).

These prophetic forecastings show that the imaginative garb gave the proactive writer the much-needed freedom to express her views in a country where creative artists were not free from punitive measures. As a keen observer of political life in South Africa, Gordimer turns a visionary in predicting the political events. She forewarned about the possible outcomes of the cruel laws of apartheid. <u>July's People</u>, set in the future, followed the fortunes of a white family who, as civil war breaks out, become dependent on their black servant. It was Gordimer's personal belief that South Africa was lucky to avoid this scenario. Whites were fortunate enough to escape the fate of the Smales because blacks were magnanimous enough to let them live. Only because of the policies of their peace-loving leader Nelson Mandela, could they survive. She has told in an interview for <u>The Telegraph</u>: "We were like lemmings, the whites, rushing to the precipice. It's a tremendous tribute to blacks in South Africa that they didn't rise up and cut all of our throats. But without Mandela it would never have happened. One doesn't know how to value Mandela enough"(1). Gordimer believed that the white man's sins were horrible enough to deserve such a predicament as that of the Smales'. Some of her visions of future South Africa are the following:

- Women will play an active role in putting an end to apartheid. Rosa Burger, Vera Stark, Hillela, and Aila are examples.

- Inter-racial marriages will see that the union of black and white races will pave the way for an entirely new 'rainbow' race. Old differences will be forgotten and the future will be free of prejudices. A Sport of Nature portrays the possibility of such a South Africa.

- She also predicted that there would be a South Africa where blacks would rule and whites would have to live at their mercy unless they look after blacks' interests. She admonishes whites to be prepared for such an eventuality as a reversal of situations. This reversal of fortunes is symbolically denoted in July's People.

- Liberal whites will not succeed in eliminating apartheid. This can be attained only through radical means. This point of view can be seen in Burger's Daughter and My Son's Story. These novels clearly depict the firm conviction of the author that only revolutionary means can achieve a solution to racial discrimination.

The author, through her works, campaigned against human rights violations. Gordimer was the first woman writer of South Africa to air her strong political and moral views. Her novels open up a window to the rest of the world through which the world can view the human rights violations in South Africa. She stands out as a humanist in spite of her preoccupation with documenting the cases of inhuman laws in South Africa. Nobel Academy has stated in Nobel Laureate biography that Gordimer through her magnificent epic writing has–in the words of Alfred Nobel–been of very great benefit to humanity.

South African situation is unique because the state itself was playing havoc with people's lives and liberty. "What Were You Dreaming?" is a short story in which a young native gets a free ride in the car driven by an Englishman who is quite new to the place. His companion briefs him about the various legal acts, which are only euphemisms for inequality:

> She has explained Acts, Proclamations, Amendments. The Group Areas
> Act, Resettlement Act, Orderly Movement, and Settlement of Black
> Persons Act. She has translated these statute-book euphemisms: people
> as movable goods. People packed onto trucks along with their stoves and
> beds while front-end loaders scoop away their homes into rubble. People
> dumped somewhere else. ("Jump" 219)

There are other subtle forms of human rights violation. When children ought to be in schools, they are found in streets learning to be slogan-shouters and demonstrators. In the short story "Comrades" Mrs. Hattie Telford happens to be a host to a group of young school dropouts. They are blacks and she is a white. She talks to a student-spokesman of the group of activists.

> —Are you still at school, Dumile?–of course, he is not at school–they are
> not at school, youngsters their age have not been at school for several
> years, they are the children growing up into young men and women for
> whom school is a battle ground, a place of boycotts and demonstrations,
> the literacy of political rhetoric, the education of revolt against having to
> live the life their parents live. They have pompous titles of responsibilities
> beyond childhood: he is the chairman of his branch of the Youth
> Congress. ("Jump" 95)

In South Africa, human rights were violated when children were denied their childhood. Gordimer's works show that she was touched by the human predicament as she found it in her country. Speaking about racism alone would have been pure ideological writing. Although most of her writings border on the political, the situations are so presented that it is hard to miss the human complexities.

Looking at the themes one by one will help one to perceive the intense texture of Gordimer's fiction. There is a common thread running through all her works and that is her humanism. Humanism is the dominant theme cutting across all the other subjects. Her vast learning and her grasp of the forces behind life have enabled her to see the human side of the conflict. She has tried to look at life's myriad colours and recorded her insights. Gordimer says in an interview with Rossouw, "The best that is within me, anything worthwhile in me, is in the books. Not in an autobiographical fashion. But I'm talking about the insights, the effort to understand life and to transpose it" (2).

It is very important to analyze a writer of her stature from the point of view of 'historical situatedness', or 'historical embedment' as it is called by Hans Bertens (79). It is pertinent to consider to what extent her novels are the products of the historical period in which they were written. It is relevant to study to what degree the socio-economic and political changes find a place in her fiction. Gordimer has analyzed the diseased political situation of her country. She has offered different perspectives on the apartheid rule including that of its supporters. Though the historical and political study is a traditional approach to literature, Gordimer fits into this criterion as she has caused amelioration in the human conditions. The most prominent feature of her writing is to study the human being as he emerges through history. To quote Wettenhall,

There is a progressive radicalization in her novels but her ideology remains essentially liberal and humanist. For the historian her work is a valuable source of information on liberalism and radicalism since 1948, but it is her sympathy for the efforts of her characters to keep a small part of their lives separate from that marks her most truly as a writer and raises her work above the level of documentary. (44)

Her humanism vitalized her to speak against the policy of apartheid even under the most adverse circumstances. Therefore, humanism is the dominant force behind all her massive literary output.

Gordimer's important themes can be summed up under political/social questions and personal/individual issues. Under the former category fall the themes like interracial tensions, feeling of insecurity by the whites, predictions about the future South Africa, emerging native women, marginalization and victimization, violence and human rights violations, binaries of master-servant, ruler-ruled, the affluent and the wretched, liberalism and radicalism, waiting for an imminent political change and the sleepless white conscience. She is a spokesperson for the issues of displacement, estrangement and immigration. Under the personal/individual category of themes fall the topics of conflict in the family, individuals finding their identity, interpersonal relationships and the impact of the political situation on personal lives, cross- racial relationships, homosexuality and lesbianism. The list, however, is not exhaustive.

Gordimer's preoccupation with the political is widely acclaimed. Gordimer never tries to escape from reality. She has tried to portray the political reality of her country on a canvas whose grand scale has not been matched by any other novelist. Women novelists are not a rarity, but women political novelists are a rarity. English women novelists in the 19th century were concerned more with the themes of the domestic front than with those of the political and ideological front. However, necessity is the mother of new themes as well. When women novelists were placed in unusual and uneasy political and social circumstances, they had to relegate the themes of intimate familial relationship to the background and had to foreground themes centring on injustice and oppression. Gordimer has captured the extraordinary political surrounds from which there was no getaway. She has presented the social and political history of South Africa through the depiction of her characters' lives. She has described the hardships of blacks as well as the relationship between different races.

Having studied the general themes of the works of Gordimer, the following chapter views her works from a postcolonial perspective.

Chapter - IV

A Chord of Racial Harmony: Mediating Between the Self and the Other

> White people are white people,
>
> They must learn to listen.
>
> Black people are black people,
>
> They must learn to talk. (Serote. qtd. in Walder 176)

Postcolonial theories refer to a set of theories in philosophy, film, art and literature that grapple with the legacy of colonial rule. As a literary theory or critical approach, it deals with literature produced in countries that were once colonies of other countries, especially the major European colonial powers such as Britain, France and Spain; in some contexts, it may include also countries still under colonial arrangements. Postcolonialism also refers to the social, political, economic and cultural practices that arise in response and resistance to colonialism. Colonialism is outdated in the ex-colonies; postcolonialism is the aftermath of colonialism; its influences are continuing.

Definition.

Postcolonial literature revalues the colonial ideology. It records the other side of the colonized or the resistance of the colonized to the colonial perception of the erstwhile slaves. Postcolonial studies rewrite the history and culture of the colonized. The motive was to react to the image created by the stranger. According to postcolonial theorists, the master discourses created by the colonizers were one-sided. When the colonized regained their tongue and when they became independent, they spoke out their perception. They rewrote their own history negating the perception of themselves as found in the Western language. Bill Ashcroft and Pal Ahluwalia write that postcolonial theories investigate, and develop propositions about the cultural and political impact of European conquest upon colonized societies, and the nature of those societies' responses.

> The 'post' in the term refers to "after colonialism began' rather than "after colonialism ended," because the cultural struggles between imperial and dominated societies continue into the present. Post-colonial theory is concerned with a range of colonial engagements: the impact of imperial languages upon colonized societies; the effects of European 'master-discourses' such as history and philosophy; the nature and consequence of colonial education and the links between Western knowledge and colonial power. (15)

The authors further state that the colonized societies invented new discourse to represent their side. In the process, they negated the Western culture and the Western language. They made innovations in the use of the language to portray the local culture as effectively as possible. Therefore, there flourished literatures written by the colonized in the colonial language.

The postcolonial writers began to rewrite their own discourse to represent themselves in a new light. Ashcroft and Ahluwalia define the function of postcolonialism thus: "In particular, it is concerned with the responses of the colonized: the struggle to control self-representation, through the appropriation of the dominant languages, discourses and forms of narratives: the struggle to present a local reality to a global audience" (15).

According to Paul Hamilton, postcolonialism is "the revaluation of Western culture's conception of itself in the light of the repressed history of exploitation of 'other' peoples on which Western economic well-being and distribution of wealth is based" (192). Postcolonialism is a direct blow on the smug Western complacency. Postcolonial criticism is sceptical about the liberal Western notions of moral and political justice. Postcolonialism also brought to light the fact that empires were built historically on the foundations of iniquitous colonial practices. Postcolonial theories also try to "reformulate more plausible concepts for understanding what actually took place under colonialism, redeeming past events from colonial ideologies of improvement and liberation and evolving new categories for mapping a resistant world from the colonized point of view" (Hamilton 193).

Before attempting a detailed study of postcolonialism, this chapter seeks to define colonialism first. Colonialism is the study of the dominance of a strong nation over a weaker nation; it is the result of a power-craving nation's desire to expand outside its own boundary. "Modern colonialism did more than extract tribute, goods and wealth from the countries that it conquered–it restructured the economies of the latter, drawing them into a complex relationship with their own, so that there was a flow of human and natural resources between colonized and colonial countries" (Loomba 9).

The colonialists were under the conviction that they were standing on high moral grounds. In defence of his wrong doings, the colonizer assumed that he was the saviour of the colonized people whom he considered as savages in need of education and civilization. The colonizer felt it was his moral duty to educate the colonized and to rehabilitate their crude culture, which was in need of repair. According to the colonizer, the colonized people lacked managerial and administrative skills, which he possessed in abundance. When the colonizer found that these people had different religious beliefs that were contradictory to his beliefs, he took upon himself the moral duty of bringing these stray people to the right path. Only these assumptions and unassailable conviction made the white Europeans venture into Africa and Asia to subjugate these natives. They made inroads into their subjects' cultures and languages, plundered their wealth and ruled over them.

In literature, the colonizer projected a stereotyped image of the colonized. According to the colonizer, the Oriental people were no better than savages were. David Huddart says that one explanation has often been the supposed inferiority of the colonized people. "Through racist jokes, cinematic images, and other forms of representation, the colonizer circulates stereotypes about the laziness or stupidity of the colonized population" (35).

Because of colonialism, the colonized culture faced total or partial erosion. The colonized were in danger of losing their identity and their uniqueness. Some people among the colonized began to react violently against the colonizer by rejecting everything that was Western. One more consequence of colonization was that the world was divided into first, second and third world countries. Next, colonialism gave birth to several forms of fundamentalism that aim at purging the local cultures of the colonial influences of the past.

Edward Said maintained that the Westerner consciously created the divide between the East and the West. The Orient is a mere textual construct. The West was conceived as the centre distinctly demarcated from the 'other'. Said stressed the need for writing back to the centre.

According to Said, the Orientalists exerted their power by 'knowing' the Orient. This knowing itself constituted power and an exercise of power. People of the Orient need to resist this power in two ways: first, by knowing the Orient outside the discourse of Orientalism, second, by representing and presenting this new knowledge to the Orientalists. He called this writing back to the empire.

There were two consequences of colonialism. One was the emergence of the new bourgeois class of people who fashioned themselves after the colonizers. Another consequence was the strong sense of national unity among the natives.

The term' colonialism' has come to acquire far more different meanings, political overtones and emotional implications than it did in the previous centuries. It has even been extended to the relations between men and women. Here, women are relegated to the position of 'other', 'marginalized' and, metaphorically speaking, colonized. Women may belong to the imperial society, yet they have to fight against male domination. In this sense, there is colonization within the imperial society.

However, in normal contexts, the term colonialism conjures up images of exploitation and repression. The term 'colonialism' is embedded in the term 'postcolonialism'. It is, therefore, conclusive that there are residues of colonialism in postcolonialism. Postcolonial period is not without the reminders of the colonial period. The literal colonizer was gone; yet, the metaphoric colonizer replaced him. This trend necessitates exploring the term 'neocolonialism'.   neocolonialism

117

Neocolonialism, according to <u>Oxford Advanced Learners' Dictionary</u>, is "the use of economic or political pressure by powerful countries to control or influence other countries." Some developed countries exercise their powers over weaker nations by controlling them in internal matters, trade and commerce and defence policies. Some of the Western countries have to pay a heavy price for their neocolonial activities. Recent attacks by suicide bombers on important targets in the US and in London are examples of subversive activities of the fundamentalist groups. These reactions are seen as the echoes of neocolonial power structures. The common threads connecting them together are exploitation and repression.

Apart from the significant contribution of Said to the postcolonial thought, there are other distinguished participants in the postcolonial discourse. Some other founding works on the theme include Frantz Fanon's <u>The Wretched of the Earth</u> and <u>Black Skin, White Masks</u>, Albert Memmi's <u>The Coloniser and the Colonised</u>, Kwame Nkruma's <u>Consciencism</u> and Aime Cesaire's <u>Discourse on Colonialism</u>. Bill Ashcroft, Gareth Griffiths, Ranjit Guha, Ngugi Wa Thiong'o, Aruna Srivatsava, Helen Tiffin, and Gayatri Spivak are the other significant contributors. Some major literary figures in postcolonial literature are Chinua Achebe, Homi Bhabha, Buchi Emecheta, Jamaica Kinkaid, Salman Rushdie and Wole Soyinka. A more comprehensive list would include Anita Desai, Amitav Ghosh, Gordimer, Bessie Head, V. S. Naipaul, Gabriel Okara, Ezekiel Mphalele, Arundati Roy, Shyam Selvadurai, Vikram Seth, Derek Walcott and a host of others.

Postcolonialism deals with an ex-colony's experiences under colonial rule. In addition, some native writers attempt to reveal distinctly their unique national and cultural identity in postcolonial literatures. African writers who imitate their native oral tradition in their English works are examples of such writers. The period dealt with in such literature is not strictly the one immediately following the end of colonial rule. Postcolonialism does not rigidly follow the chronological aftermath of the foreign rule.

Postcolonial situation has different faces in different contexts. The erstwhile colonies are divided into settler countries and non-settler countries. Australia and Canada are examples of settler countries. India, Sri Lanka, Jamaica, and Nigeria are examples of non-settler countries. The position of countries such as Zimbabwe and South Africa is not as simple as this.

In South Africa, the decolonization process ended with a new type of postcolonization–apartheid. South Africa has to be approached as an example for postcolonial oppression. The neocolonizers took up the new weapon of apartheid to exploit the ex-colony. The perpetrators of this cruel law were the immigrant Afrikaner settlers. Therefore, anticolonilism in the South African context is synonymous with anti-apartheid movement. Apartheid literally meant 'Separate development.' Though the meaning of the term sounds harmless in Dutch, the law robbed the blacks of their rights.

Having situated South Africa in the postcolonial context, the study now focuses on the application of the various aspects of postcolonialism to the novels of Gordimer.

Binarism is a postcolonial concept deserving attention in detail. Binarism means a pair, two or dualism. It is a principle of opposition of two ideas or concepts. In any

Binarism

119

society, such oppositions are very common. These oppositions establish a relation of dominance. Because of the co-existence of opposing binaries, one tends to dominate the other. The most common binaries are black and white, men and women, civilized and primitive, educated and illiterate, rich and poor, master and servant, liberal and radical, developed and underdeveloped, personal and political among other things.

Postcolonialism views the Oriental and the Westerner as two distinct opposites. This opposition was used to justify the white man's destiny to rule the naturally subordinate Orientals. Gordimer's works deal with all the opposites perceived between blacks and whites.

Many of her novels deal with an individual's preoccupation with the personal and the political. Of her novels, Burger's Daughter and My Son's Story are telling examples of the dilemma between the personal and the political. Any individual is a creature of the circumstances according to the Marxian critic, Georg Lukács, who feels that there is no life for individuals divorced from community. In his article on Gordimer, Dominic Head states that the writings of the Marxist critic Georg Lukács have been an important influence on Gordimer. He further says that Lukács' notion of typification in the portrayal of characters has influenced the manner in which she examines the interaction of the private and public realms.

For Lukács, character ought to be a representation, simultaneous of individuality and historical typification. Gordimer's vision of typicality reaches a peak in Burger's Daughter (1979) where the life of the central character Rosa Burger runs parallel to the history of modern South Africa.

> Rosa is held as typical figure, representative of the white population by
> virtue of her complicity, but also through her eventful resolve to become a
> political subversive. (2)

She is a typical South African white, yet her individuality emerges when she resolves to enter public life.

Polarities or binaries exist in other forms, too. For example, loyalty and betrayal coexist in My Son's Story. While Sonny is loyal to his conviction to fight against apartheid until the end, he betrays his wife by having an illegal relationship with a white woman. His strong commitment to the cause in the public sphere and his weak surrender to the bodily desires form the polarized conflict from which he cannot escape. His obsession with 'needing Hannah' is his tragic flaw leading to his fall.

Love and violence are the next binaries co-existing in a person. This phenomenon can be extended to the society. The House Gun is a morally complex novel set in the liberated South Africa. A white murderer depends on a black lawyer to find out the legal loopholes that will let him escape. Duncan murders a man he loves out of jealousy. The reason why this act was possible can be traced to the society. The South African Whites, out of fear, possessed guns to safeguard themselves. Whenever such passions as jealousy are aroused, the gun comes in handy. The story sadly recalls the fact that if the house gun had not been around, as it generally is, in white families, the murder would not have happened. In several developed countries, even the loved ones fall prey to the "house gun" simply because of its easy availability.

Stephen Clingman, a critic on Gordimer's works, has traced the binaries in her novels in his article, "Surviving Murder: Oscillation and Triangulation in Gordimer's The House Gun." He argues that The House Gun presents the binaries in the sudden dislocation of the white couple Claudia and Harald. When their son Duncan commits a murder, they find themselves dependent on the black lawyer Hamilton Motsamai. The reality is too much for the couple to bear. Claudia and Harald belong to the class of wealthy whites, whereas Motsamai, the lawyer, has risen from the world of impoverishment and exile. Motsamai is "now the figure of wealth and authority whose presence and voice they must come to trust" (Clingman140).

Again, there is the binary of demure woman bound by homely duties and participatory woman responding to the call of the nation. This conflict finds a resolution in two remarkable women in Gordimer's novels: Aila and Rosa. In Aila, the resolution springs as a surprise whereas in Rosa it is a synthesis after a long debate within herself. In a country with conflicts like South Africa, anything is possible. Characters are unpredictable; anyone could be a spy or a revolutionary involved in the clandestine movement.

For example, in the short story "A Chip of Glass Ruby," Bamjee is baffled when his wife is arrested in the middle of the night for her secret revolutionary activities. "I don't understand how she can do the things she does when her mind is always full of woman's non-sense at the same time—that's what I don't understand with her" (Six Feet of the Country 46). The same mysterious transformation takes place in Aila in My Son's Story. In Burger's Daughter, the oppositional forces at work in Rosa's mind are "the self–regarding life" and "the public orientation" (Peck, "One Foot" 32).

In <u>A Guest of Honour</u>, the binaries are present in the form of neocolonialism and trade unionism represented by Mweta and Shinza respectively. Mweta is the leader of a newly independent African country. Shinza, an erstwhile supporter of Mweta turns an opponent when Mweta's politics becomes neocolonial. Shinza supports trade unions, which Mweta tries to suppress with an iron hand. Colonialism is outdated, yet other conflicting binaries exist in the independent states.

Clingman also traces the patterns of binaries in <u>The Conservationist</u>. According to him, the central binary pattern emerges in the relationship between Mehring and the black body buried shallowly. This binary poses the question of `possession' which is answered in the end. Mehring is forced to leave the farm whereas the resurrected body is given a proper burial by the black community that has taken hold of the farm.

Mehring's attitude towards blacks is typical of the Afrikaners. He tries to dismiss the death of the black man in a factual manner. He thinks of the abject poverty in the location that leads to murders and killings. "The poor devil–that other poor devil–is dead anyway. In that enormous location these things happen every day . . . they are murdered for their Friday pay-packets or they simply stab each other after drinking" (<u>Conser</u>. 28). It was usual to talk about and to treat blacks as thieves and rogues. Mehring's friend asks him whether there are instance of stock-theft when he enquires him about safety on the farm. Mehring replies, "I haven't lost anything yet but an old chap, De Beer, reckons to lose a couple of head a year. In spite of his dogs. And his reputation for shooting on sight" (<u>Conser</u>. 30).

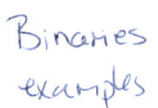
Binaries
examples

Clingman also suggests that there are multiple binaries in <u>Burger's Daughter</u>. Rosa has imaginary dialogues with her father, her lover, her father's first wife Katya and the young black man, Bassie. In <u>July's People</u>, the binary relationship is between Maureen and July. Stephen Clingman says, "We might say that such binary patterns have been in Gordimer's work virtually from the beginning" (143).

The binaries of Western materialism and the Eastern spiritualism are vibrant in <u>The Pickup</u>, one of Gordimer's latest works. Julie is tired of the materialism of the West. She now understands what it means to live in a family guided by the Islamic code. She learns to live in poverty and backwardness. She teaches English to the women in a remote Arab village and earns her livelihood. She reads the Quran and grows to appreciate her mother-in-law's spiritual life. She is taken in by the desert though her husband considers her tryst with the desert as silly romanticism.

The binaries of the rich South African youth and the poor Arab youth are present in the novel. The South African youth do not live under threat anymore. This is post apartheid period and there is no danger but only boredom. Julie is tired of wealth and success whereas Ibrahim craves for permanent residence in one of the western countries. Julie finds satisfaction in restriction and hardships whereas Ibrahim is ashamed of the poverty and backwardness of his village. With this novel, Gordimer has reached a new height thematically. She has touched geographically and philosophically hitherto untouched areas.

Marginality is the next postcolonial term that needs mentioning in the context of Gordimer's fiction. Centre represents power and those who are on the periphery or

Marginality

margins have no access to power. Those who live on the margins are out of reach of affluence and influence. Marginality is the result of the binaristic structure of various kinds of dominance such as patriarchy, imperialism, and caste system. Certain forms of experiences are peripheral because of the existence of these dominant forces. Ashcroft, Griffiths and Tiffin define marginality in The Key Concepts in the Postcolonial Studies: "Marginal, therefore, indicates a positionality that is best defined in terms of the limitations of a subject's access to power" (135).

Marginalization resulted in 'othering.' M.S. Nagarajan says that the two terms are interrelated, one begetting the other. To quote M.S. Nagarajan,

> The colonizers were the centre, 'the self', and the colonized were the margins, 'the other'. This is the practice of 'othering', going by names such as 'the demonic other,' or the 'exotic other.' It is the result of the long-held arrogant and supercilious belief in the racial superiority of the Caucasian over the Asiatic. This attitude, of raising the European culture as the ultimate standard by which to measure the other culture, is designated Eurocentricism which employs what is called the philosophy of 'universalism'. (186)

Some of Gordimer's characters exhibit the Eurocentric views. For example, when Margot Wentz's cooks want to be pilots, she scoffs at them as if it is not legitimate for blacks to aspire to fly planes. Blacks are supposed to wallow in poverty and only whites could climb up the social and economic ladder.

The apartheid law pushed the blacks, the coloured, and the Indians to the brink. The Afrikaners also marginalized the other South African whites. The whole of Gordimer's writing career starting from the 1940s until the rescinding of apartheid coincided with the political marginalization of the white English-speaking South African community. This community found it increasingly difficult to align with the Afrikaner nationalism though a majority finally sided with them. Afrikaners made it more and more difficult for blacks, who began to distance themselves from the white South Africans. The apartheid law prevented any kind of socialization between blacks and whites. Gordimer was an insider writing about the trauma of the marginalized English-speaking whites.

Postcolonial period also witnesses how the old margins blur yielding place to new. The novels <u>The House Gun</u> and <u>The Pickup</u> depict the flux within marginalization. For example, Hamilton Motsomai, a famous black lawyer who occupies an enviable status now, lived on the fringes of the society during his boyhood. After reaching the elevation, Motsomai condescends to help Abdu, the marginalized friend of Julie. Surprisingly, Motsomai, too, resents Julie's choice to marry a poor Arab youth. This shows that in spite of the demolition of apartheid, other forms of margins exist. Instead of colour, now, eminence and success put a person at the centre.

Marginalization within the marginalized societies is something more tragic. For example, women were doubly marginalized in the patriarchal white society. In a number of short stories, Gordimer equates the white woman's predicament with that of the blacks. Her short stories "Six Feet of the Country", "Is There No Where Else Where We Can Meet", "Good Climate and Friendly Inhabitants" and "A Soldier's Embrace" clearly show how the white woman identifies herself with the blacks on the margin. "Town Lovers," "Country Lovers" and "Oral History" are stories that describe the sad plight of black women because of the Immorality Act and its shabby and partial execution. Martin Trump says, "Gordimer achieves a fascinating identification between the white women and the black people who feature in them; she perceives and describes connections and common factors in their victimizations" (364).

Gordimer's works, in a sense, gave voice to the voiceless. The 'voiceless' are the miniscule minority of whites who sided with the blacks. She pays tribute or does justice *white* to those whites who were not afraid to speak for the blacks. Her works offer a view into *conscience* the workings of the white conscience. Black writers were too preoccupied with their plight to bother about the participation of whites in the struggles and its ramifications on their familial life. However, Gordimer used her works to forewarn the South African whites about the possible consequences of the continued oppression of the blacks. Her novels stand as a testimony to the role of writers in the event of repressive regimes. The racial advantage did not deter her from viewing apartheid as an evil. She visits the by-lanes of apartheid and provides a balanced view of apartheid.

The increased power of some black men and women alters the nature of the white female-black male relationship, whether at a conscious or a subconscious level. Vera Stark has a special but not sexual relationship with the black leader Zeph Rapulana. Although Gordimer denies that Zeph's blackness is important, Vera Stark's bond with him derives from his having risked his life in a black squatters' confrontation with a white farmer. Furthermore, Vera's abandoned white husband knows that, by living in an "annexe" to

127

Zeph's house, Vera is on "the safest kind of premises, in present conditions, the property of a prominent black man [now in finance] not overtly involved in " (None 321-22). Whites become increasingly dependent on blacks. This speaks volumes of the success made by the independent and intelligent blacks.

Among her longer fictional works, Hillela in A Sport of Nature is able to build a rapport with her black lovers because she is able to identity their position in the larger scheme of things. Hillela is brought up by her activist-aunt and she closely follows the incidents happening around her.

> Changes in her personal life run parallel to the various steps being taken by the blacks against the white regime. Her social consciousness is awakened repeatedly by the report of police torture, beating, electric shocks, and extended denial of sleep to the black activists. Through the events around her Hillela arrives at an understanding of self. The pretty girl is foot-loose. The ruptured kinships and displaced marginal emotions make her an exile. She finds herself in the middle of the African cause. (Shinde 96)

This shows how Hillela's own life on the margins enables her to lead the fight for the cause of the blacks.

"The Ultimate Safari" a short story in the collection "Jump" and other Stories presents the extreme consequences of marginalization. It is an ironic tale of a black family who are on the move to another village. On the way, they have to avoid being seen by whites. They have to perform such an arduous journey that they envy the animals that had a better lot than themselves. The small girl in "The Ultimate Safari" juxtaposes humans and animals, which the girl observes, are roaming freely in their habitat with enough to eat–while she and others are forced to flee and go hungry.

> We followed the animals to where they drank. When they had gone, we
> went to their water holes. We were never thirsty without finding water, but
> the animals ate at all the times. Whenever you saw them, they were eating,
> grass, trees, roots. And there was nothing for us. The mealies were
> finished. The only food we could eat was what the baboons ate, dry little
> figs full of ants that grew along the branches of trees at the rivers. It was
> hard to be like the animals. ("Jump" 38)

Citing one or two examples for marginality in Gordimer's fiction is far from satisfactory.

Gordimer identified herself with the causes of the black marginalized people of her country, yet she was socially removed from them. A few of her novels offer a prophetic vision of the future Africa where there will be justice for blacks. Her stories are written in an elitist style and the point of view is most often that of an elite white man or woman. Martin Trump has made this observation:

> Gordimer's writing can be seen as evidence of her paradoxical social
> position: a white person living in privilege in South Africa, feted by an

international readership and yet espousing the causes of the deprived black

South African masses. The ideological implications of her works are

populist, and yet their forum and mode of expression are elitist. (343)

Though her novels are stylistically at the centre catering to an elite readership, her
concern was for those on the margins.

Miscegenation.

Miscegenation is another postcolonial feature. It is the sexual union of different
races specifically whites and blacks. This issue had always haunted the white colonizers
and their settler descendents. They always wanted to maintain the purity of the races.
The infamous Immorality Act punished those who had such relationships. This law hunted
down those whites who had either marital or sexual liaison with people from other races.
The colonizers were obsessed with the elimination of the products of such unions. Despite
the law, there was attraction between the races. However, at the end of such relationships,
always the blacks were at a disadvantage. Invariably, at the end of the trials the court
acquitted white sinners. Yet, A Sport of Nature explores the possibility of fruitful unions
between blacks and whites as a potential way of bridging the gap between the races.

"Other" is another postcolonial term usually associated with the marginalized
groups. "Other" refers to those colonized subjects who are identified by their difference
from the centre. They become "the focus of anticipated mastery of the imperial ego"
(Ashcroft, Griffiths, and Tiffin, Key 170). The identification and this ability to enter the
other made Gordimer create a character like Hillela.

Gordimer is a white writing about the 'other.' It is relevant to study her novels with a view to find whether her writings express the superiority of whites over the natives. Gordimer emerged from the colonial race. It is pertinent to read her novels with a view to find whether she harboured the notion that "the natives were uncivilized, lacking morals, and the Anglo-Europeans must educate them, because they were advanced in life" (Nagarajan 186). Reading her novel from a postcolonial perspective reveals the fact that Gordimer embraced the other and held sympathetic views about the other. However, Margot Wentz in A Guest of Honour argues that blacks had to suffer in order to be civilized with all the modern amenities. Bray, the anti-colonial spokesperson of Gordimer, observes both the points of view. He appreciates and applauds the non-racial view held by Rebecca and the like. Margot Wentz is not Gordimer's spokesperson. Her text is anti-colonialist, as most of her protagonists are.

Alterity is the next postcolonial term popularized by Bakhtin. This is the state of being other or different. It refers to "the way in which an author moves away from identification with a character" (Ashcroft, Griffiths, and Tiffin, Key 16). Gordimer has acknowledged that it is impossible for a black to understand a white completely just as it is impossible for a white to understand a black completely. She herself was a writer trying to capture the multifaceted life of South Africa. Whom does she identify with? What is the role of whites in a country where blacks are the majority? There were also questions of negritude and black consciousness, which denied any positive role for whites. She does not take sides. Her concern is with suffering, be it whites or blacks.

Even though most of her chief characters are whites, Gordimer had the unassailable faith that apartheid was a wrong policy. This conviction led her imagination to devise

131

ways and means of escaping the stronghold of apartheid. One of her weapons was hybridity. She argues tacitly through one of her novels that trying to become the 'other' will solve the problem of apartheid largely. Through hybrid marriages, this dream may come true. In A Sport of Nature, she portrays the main character Hillela as capable of understanding the other. She suggests through her character that life would be successful for the minority whites if they developed the capability of entering the consciousness of the other. Robin Visel says, "In Charlotte Bronte and Jean Rhys, in Oliver Schreiner and Doris Lessing, and above all in Gordimer, the discovery of the other, the venture into blackness, is fertilizing, liberating and self-actualizing" (36).

Rebecca Edwards of A Guest of Honour has something in common with Hillela. Rebecca decides to send her children to a South African school. Here, in the independent Central African nation, she feels at home sharing a house with a black family, the Tlumes. Bray questions her decision to send her children to South Africa where apartheid laws prevail. Does she know her children will grow up in South Africa with a colonial mindset? "Here you are all living happily with the Tlumes. And you'll send them there, to be brought up in the antiquated colonial way, to consider that their white skin sets them above other people" (Guest 235). Rebecca replies, "Well, what about me? It was like that in Kenya. It's only while they're at school; they'll grow out of it again" (Guest 235). Bray says to Rebecca, "You cling to reality. They couldn't condition you into the good old colonial abstractions–a nigger's a nigger and a white man's an English gentleman. You obstinately stick to the other criteria–I don't know what they are, but they certainly aren't based on colour" (Guest 235). For Rebecca and Hillela, getting into the other is easy.

Gordimer calls such people as realists who cannot be without principles. Rebecca's deep convictions make her send her children to South Africa and still believe that her children will be immune to the colonial background just as she had been.

A hybrid culture is a postcolonial phenomenon. It is the "aftermath of imperialism" (Ashcroft, Griffiths, and Tiffin, Key 10). The authors further state: "Post-colonial cultures are inevitably hybridized, involving a dialectical relationship between European ontology and epistemology and the impulse to create and recreate independent local identity" (95). Hillela is the new type of revolutionary who wants to create a rainbow-coloured nation for her children. Visel says that Hillela is the white colonial female character who can identify with blackness in a more creative and pronouncing manner to achieve greatness. "For her alone among Gordimer's heroines, blackness is not alien, but rather her native element" (Visel 39).

The success story of Hillela reminds one of Gordimer's own decision to stay on in South Africa and fulfil her literary dreams. Gordimer herself did not flee the oppressive white governments. She did not seek refuge in one of the European countries. She could identify blackness in herself, so she was able to stay. Robert Visel identifies Gordimer with two of her characters:

> While not an autobiographical character, Hillela, like Gordimer's other heroines, is a vehicle for personal statement. Through Rosa she affirms her own commitment to remaining in South Africa as witness and

activist. . . . Through Hillela she signals her disassociation from what she sees as the dead values of the past, imaginatively reinventing a new personality to fit a new country. (40)

Though Hillela is an amoral and unconventional character, Gordimer seems to suggest that a positive future is possible for the white South Africans only with the help of people like Hillela who will bridge the gap between the past and the future.

Cami Hewett has commented on the pristine status of hybrid persons thus: "A hybrid person, then, becomes neither purely native nor wholly colonialist, nor even a mix of the two. Rather, through mutual influence, the hybrid individual creates a pristine place in which to reside and revolutionize the accepted standards of the culture and the colonist" (62). Through Hillela, Gordimer dreams of a rainbow nation where black and white and colours in between merge to form different hues. Gordimer has used A Sport of Nature as a vehicle for delivering the message that only by entering the 'other', reconciliation would be possible in South Africa.

'Ambivalence' is another postcolonial characteristic put forth by Homi Bhabha. About ambivalence Ashcroft, Griffiths, and Tiffin write: "It describes the complex mix of attraction and repulsion that characterizes the relationship between the colonizer and the colonized. The relationship is ambivalent because the colonized subject is never simply and completely opposed to the colonizer" (Key 14-15). This ambivalence is clearly brought out in A Sport of Nature through the distress of Hillela's cousin Sasha. Sasha wonders why he is required to enrol in the army after his school. His parents send him to a school with black kids. His father defends blacks in the court and his mother is an activist fighting for their rights. Nevertheless, the law of the land requires him to go into the army and learn to kill blacks.

A fine example for the attitude of liberal whites is the character of a white doctor in A Sport of Nature. The doctor helped the white lawyer Joe win a case on behalf of a black man by giving vital testimony of torture. He describes the appalling findings on the man's body and adds in the same breath: "By the way, Joe . . . while you were appearing in Durban, were you ever invited to the Club? I was given a surprisingly good lunch there . . . charming place, lovely old colonial style . . . really enjoyed it" (113). Pauline wonders how he is able to reconcile the two–his being a witness to brutality in the morning and enjoying lunch at a white club.

Some blacks were submissive and conformist in their attitude towards the policy of the rulers. The Ambassador's family in A Sport of Nature give refuge to Hillela because they feel her position as an exile with protectors might be useful to them. Hillela's black leader-lover was a prize-guest for them. The family of the Ambassador think that the colonial rulers have programmed blacks in a way they want them to talk. Talking to them does not reveal any understanding about them. This is why even the sympathetic liberals are not positively disposed towards blacks. The ambassador and his wife did not usually entertain blacks other than those who were unavoidable through protocol: "What pleasure is there? I don't see the point of mixing just because they are black. What can you talk about with them? They serve us up with platitudes they think we want to hear because that's what white people taught them. You never know what they think. Never give anything of themselves" (Sport 173).

Colonialism had two sides, both for the colonizer and the colonized. For the colonized, colonialism also meant modernization along with the repression. For the colonizer in Europe, slaves were also imported along with precious metals. The impact of the imperialism was complex, indeed. On the one hand, it caused tremendous damage to indigenous cultures and a lot of suffering and loss to the colonized. The irreparable loss to the colonized is the instilling of the feeling of inferiority based on their colour. For the colonizer, there existed no culture, history, and value outside their own frame. Dennis Walder refers to the ambivalence of colonialism in the following words:

> On the other hand, the constructive or at least modernizing effects of colonial rule are apparent too–from the introduction of railways to the breaking down of taboos; from the building of schools and hospitals, to the rediscovery and revitalization of cultures. Similarly profound and ambivalent has been the impact of colonization upon Europe, from the arrival of vast quantities of precious metals in the early years, to the effects of slavery and immigration more recently. (40)

One of her early novels A World of Strangers announces the theme of ambivalence in clear terms. When Toby Hood sets out for South Africa, the members of his family are excited about the prospects of his studying the effects of apartheid in Africa. They look upon his visit as an enviable opportunity because he would be able to collect data about the minorities living in South Africa. However, their expectation that he should become "a *voyeur* of the world's ills and social perversions" (World 36) fills Toby with irritation, hostility, and resentment. That was what Gordimer as a young writer in South Africa set out do. She has portrayed life by drawing black, white and coloured characters from life and rendered them realistically on her screen.

As a white, Gordimer shares the ambivalent attitude towards blacks. Though she portrays black life sincerely, she is unable to find fault with the white race completely. She wants to depict the truth: human life with its strengths and weaknesses. Her characters are imbued with the traits of ordinary people. For example, in July's People, Maureen Smales used to treat July as one of her people. However, in his village she discovers that deep in her mind she had harboured the idea that people like July would be capable of pilfering. That is why she easily believes that July was usurping their bakkie. July also has ambivalent relationship with his masters. Though it never surfaced, July always had the grudge that he was only a 'boy'; he could never become one of them. In the city, July was dependent on the white family for everything. In his village, they depend on him for their shelter and succour. When she accuses him of hiding the whereabouts of Daniel, who has stolen their gun, he bounces back: "Me? I must know who is stealing your things? Same you always. You make too much trouble for me. Here in my home too. Daniel, the chief, my mother, my wife with the house. Trouble, trouble from you. I don't want it any more. You see?" (July 151). July who was devoted to Maureen retaliates when Maureen hurls abuse at him.

July is an instance for the empire hitting back. He had always tried to please his masters. Now, he realizes that he is judged on their own terms. He suddenly realizes that he should speak in his own tongue, not in the borrowed tongue. The colonizer will not bear if the slave begins to talk. He has behaved only to fulfil her idea of him, just in order to please her. He was judged as a man by her own standards, not by his ideas of intelligence, honesty and dignity. Her worldview is different from his, or that of his people. By switching to his own language, he emerges from the assumptions of his masters and asserts his differences. He reclaims his individuality by talking in his tongue.

> Suddenly he began to talk at her in his own language, his face flickering powerfully. The heavy cadences surrounded her; the earth was fading and a thin, far radiance from the moon was faintly thickening parachute-like hazes stretched over the sky. She understood although she knew no word. Understood everything: what he had had to be, how she had covered up to herself for him, in order for him to be her idea of him. But for himself–to be intelligent, honest, dignified for *her* was nothing. His measure as man was taken elsewhere and by others. She was not his mother, his wife, his sister, his friend, his people. (July 152)

July's decision to talk in his mother tongue is analogous to the decision of native writers to use the native idiom in their stories. They were dissatisfied with the white writer's view. Native writers like Chinua Achebe began to wield their pens to express themselves in their own idiom, after getting tired of the European view of Africans. The European world-view held the white race at the centre. Achebe and his kind will keep themselves at the centre and repudiate the alien writers who tried to cast the natives into the European mould. Achebe realised that the natives had their own stories to tell and those stories could not be told by anyone else.

There is mutual attraction and repulsion between the races though they are pitted against each other collectively. Double consciousness is a common phenomenon among whites as well as blacks. For the colonized, the colonizer's culture and life-style had been something they always wanted to emulate. My Son's Story depicts the admiration Sonny has for the white life. It has always been a dream for Sonny to live in the whites-only area. His son Will also yearns for the luxury of the white life. He goes to the cinema "to bunk study and to sit in the maroon nylon velvet seat of a cinema in a suburb where whites live" (Son 3). When Sonny decides to move to the Whites-only area, he has to allay the fears of his wife. He calls their house as a 'ghetto' or a 'hovel'. He plays upon the ambition of any coloured family to live among the whites:

> It's a nice house. Three bedrooms, a sitting room, another room we can
> use for your sewing and my books–imagine? I'll be able to have a desk.
> We'll do up the kitchen, I'll build you a breakfast nook. And there's a big
> yard. A huge old apricot tree. Will can make a tree-house. (Son 42)

This kind of admiration for a comfortable life, the sole right of the whites, led the couple to work for their community.

Their attitude is not unambiguous and simple. If Sonny hates the whites' policy, he is not without admiration for their way of life. An intellectual like Sonny cannot flourish in his chosen line because he is not a white. Though he wants very much to participate in the whites' intellectual life, he is barred from it. The author describes the anguish of Sonny at his inability to "belong to whatever cultural circles the town had–the amateur players'

[handwritten margin note: Black dilemma]

139

theatre, the chamber music society . . . the Sunday bird-watchers' group, although he was interested in nature. . . . He could not belong to the chess club. . . . He could not afford to buy many books" (Son 16).

Here, again, there is an ambiguous attitude towards the oppressor. The author ironically states that Sonny is educated enough to appreciate Shakespeare but this lover of Shakespeare never had the right to enter the municipal library. Though the educated blacks are denied access to the white culture and literary life, they aspire to live like them. The oppressed subjects are, thus, not simply and completely opposed to the oppressor. Their relationship is more complex than the simple terms of love and hatred.

Didactic

Dislocation is another postcolonial term worth mentioning. Postcolonialism is not simply decolonization, because many people living in both ex-colonies and ex-colonizing countries are still subject to the oppressions put into place by colonialism. Dislocation is one of the main problems faced by the native population. The book Key Concepts in Postcolonial Studies describes 'dislocation' thus:

> In a different sense, dislocation is also a feature of all invaded colonies
> where indigenous cultures are, if not annihilated, often literally dislocated,
> that is, moved off what was their territory. At best, they are metaphorically
> dislocated, placed into a hierarchy that sets their culture aside, ignores its
> institutions, and values in favour of the values and practices of the
> colonizing culture. Many postcolonial texts acknowledge the psychological

and personal dislocations that result from this cultural denigration, and it is against this dislocating process that many modern decolonizing struggles are instituted. (Ashcroft, Griffiths, and Tiffin 75)

None to Accompany Me discusses the issue of dislocation that affected the native population. Exile and imprisonment are the reasons for these consequences. Normal maturing process is affected in the children of the exiles. Sibongile and Didymus were black exiles once. They return to Africa with their daughter Mpho. Mpho is a bright girl who has had superior education in exile but there were no "suitable contacts for her in the dirt and violence of a place like Alexandra" (None 77). Mpho has not learnt her mother tongue properly because her parents had migrated to England when she was very young. Exiles "But English was the medium for Mpho, English was the reminder to her that there was no running away from what she was, what circumstances made of her, a girl who had to have lessons in order to claim her mother tongue"(None 186). Exiles had the cultural and psychological dislocation in addition to the literal disarticulation.

Gordimer talks about the gap in the development of Oupa and Mpho. "They both have been displaced, their relative ages don't tally naturally with their actual experiences, there's a dislocation that couldn't be corrected. He missed out his teenage stage, in jail; she has a worldly sophistication beyond her years, because of European exile" (None 177-178).

Several of Gordimer's short stories and novels portray the travails of the blacks restricted to specific areas. Their movements are curtailed and their freedom is denied. Blacks were treated like commodity and were dislocated *en masse*. Government officials

141

ordered the appropriate personnel " to bulldoze the homes of a community, pack the inhabitants and their belongings into trucks drawn, like any other government equipment, from the States' stores, and transport them to an area designated by the appropriate department" (None 12). The author also comments on the rationalization of the white government that asked the people to leave their cows and goats behind. "They might be allowed to bring along bits and ends left intact by the demolition of their houses–a window-frame or some boards–but cows and goats had to be left behind; what would the beasts feed on, in a stretch of velt cleared and levelled for the barest human occupation?" (None 13).

All industrialized nations have absorbed immigrants from other countries. The successive generations of such immigrants have shed some of their cultural heritage and acquired new cultural baggage of the host nation. It is very hard to escape such cultural and linguistic displacements. Unless there is assimilation of the alien aspects, difference is inevitable. Unless the immigrants and the natives pledge to the general liberal humanist value system, conflict is inescapable. Only a genuine interest in the welfare of the minorities will ease the threatening atmosphere.

Like other postcolonial literatures, Gordimer's fiction, too, focuses on the cultural displacements–and its effects on personal and communal identities. Her novels and short stories study the processes and effects of cultural displacement and the ways in which the culturally displaced defended themselves. Though the rulers suppressed the voices of dissent, they could not continue in their effort. Hans Bertens says,

Postcolonial theory in particular, sees such displacements, and the

ambivalences and hybrid cultural forms to which they lead, as vantage

points that allow us to expose the internal doubts and the instances of

resistance that West has suppressed in its steamrolling globalizing course

and to deconstruct the seamless façade that the combination of

imperialism and capitalism has traditionally striven to present. (200)

Gordimer reveals herself a thorough intellectual and artist. She blends

imagination and reality in A Guest of Honour in such exact proportions that the reading

of it leaves one wondering whether Gordimer had the experience of moving closely

with politicians, rulers and revolutionaries. Gordimer's grasp of the situation is so

complete and engrossing that one is overawed by her political intelligence. Her

knowledge of political theories amazes the readers. She explores new grounds by

entering the inner recesses of politics and warfare. She is an unconventional woman

writer who has explored themes that were the strongholds of men writers.

She has posited quite a few postcolonial theories in her magnificent novel,

A Guest of Honour. It is an epistemological novel with a rich repository of postcolonial ideals

and ideas. The author emerges as a postcolonial theorist by taking up for her theme

the travails of a new democracy. The novel is an impartial critique of the postcolonial

state of affairs in an erstwhile colony and hence demands detailed scrutiny.

Colonial discourses usually get self-congratulatory when they discuss their

own affairs. Hostility and aggression mark the discourse when it discusses the affairs of the 'other.' James Bray seems to be the spokesperson of the author without getting blinded by the colonial lens.

James Bray is the title figure of this heavy novel about an unnamed central African ex-colony. The damages and the ravages caused by the erstwhile colonizers and the travails of the new rulers are effectively illustrated in the novel. Bray returns to this country after a decade. He was formerly working as the District Commissioner at Gala. He had been recalled to England after the colonizers found that he supported blacks' independence struggle. Now, he has come back to attend the celebrations at the invitation of Mweta, the first black president of the country. The president presses him to stay on so that he can assist the government by assessing the educational needs of the new democracy.

Bray surveys the schools in the Gala District that he knows so well. He is appalled by the conditions of the city, the bush, and the country. Bray could sense that the country is experiencing the inevitable birth pangs of a new democracy of which the people and the rulers have no experience. The previous rulers had been too clever to provide the natives with the necessary education and knowledge to head the government. As soon as Bray settles down, he is greeted with the smells of the country. This is a symbolic representation of the ravages caused by the previous government and the efforts taken by the new government. Bray perceives both death and life in the new country.

> A rich stink of dead animal rose self-dispersed, like a gas, every now and
> then as he drank his tea, and he got up and looked around, as he had done
> so many times before, and with as little success, to see if a rat or mole
> were rotting somewhere. Whatever it was could never be found; it was the

smell of the growth, they had long ago decided, at Gala, the process of

decay and regeneration so accelerated, brought so close together that it

produced the reek of death-and-life, all at once. (Guest 13-14)

Through the many anecdotes narrated by Roly Dando, a long-time friend of Bray,

he picks up bits and pieces of real information and opinion about Mweta's position and

the sort of team he has gathered around him. Dando says, "Of course, Mweta has to hand

out a job to everybody. Every pompous jackass from the bush. . . . They're all heroes,

you know, heroes of the struggle" (Guest 15).

African countries are settler-colonies where the colonizers chose to remain after

independence. The author mentions how the former rulers have become turncoats in

order to please the new rulers. Through Roly Dando "Bray learned of the swift about-face

by which some white people turned a smile on the new regime, while others had already

packed up and left the country" (Guest 16).

In any postcolonial country, the phenomenon of mimicry is quite significant.

The same ills about which the colonized were unhappy are repeated in the new regime.

Dando describes the emerging blacks as the new 'genteel lot' and whites looking down

upon them with chagrin. "A genteel lot, very conscious of their dignity, man-about-town

and all that, you can imagine how the white toughies feel about all those white collars

round black necks in the bar" (Guest 7).

Inequality is a postcolonial phenomenon most prevalent in many countries.

"The newly independent nation-state makes available the fruits of liberation only selectively and unevenly: the dismantling of colonial rule did not automatically bring about changes for the better in the status of women, the working class or the peasantry in most colonized countries" (Loomba 16). When the blacks start ruling themselves, the same colonial problems persist. "The blacks' dirty work isn't any cleaner than the whites'" (Guest 19). Dando notes that some of his white colleagues had migrated to South Africa and Rhodesia "where they can feel confident they'll never have a black man on the bench to give verdict as biased as a white man's" (Guest 19).

The complete colonial experience of the blacks is encompassed in the words of Margot Wentz. The sympathy and good work of the British for the locals was not out of love; it was in return for the services of the blacks. Margot Wentz justifies the hardships of blacks saying that only two generations of blacks had had to experience hardships so that their progeny might live in the modern world with railways and electricity. Colonial rule was the price they had to pay in order to be ushered into the modern world.

> I am sorry, forty-eight years you were under British rule, digging their
> mines, building roads for them, making towns, living in shanties and
> waiting on them, treated like dirt–now it's all over, you really think there
> was any way at all you could enter the modern world without suffering?
> You think there was someone else who would have given you the alphabet
> and electricity and killed off the malaria mosquito, just for love?
> The Finns? Swedes? The Russians? Anybody? Anyone who wouldn't
> have wanted the last drop of your sweat and pride in return? These are the
> facts. (Guest 32-33)

Whites resent the progress made by blacks. Margot's husband Wentz had escaped

persecution in Germany. The Wentzes have sought asylum in the Central African country,

yet Margot cannot appreciate the new country. Despite the fact that they had fled Germany to

live safely in Africa, she believes that her children have grown up in an uncivilized country.

She calls her son and daughter as "such bloody yahoos" (Guest 176). Her daughter

Emmanuel points out the irony: "My *mother* wrings her hands because we've grown up

wild in Africa, so *uncultured,* without the proper intellectual training of the Europeans

who wanted to murder her" (Guest 176). They have escaped murder and mayhem in their

own country perpetrated by the so-called Europeans and live in comfort in an alien land.

Emmanuel is aware of the fact that to be in Africa she has to shed her European

superiority. Barbaric behaviour like genocide, and torture were prevalent among the

whites, too. Only those who have a wakeful conscience can generalize such facts and

sympathize with blacks.

The author describes the postcolonial situation of inadequacy to meet the needs of

the people, both educational and economic. The colonial rulers had never cared about the

independent country's destiny. There is a shortage of teachers because the colonizers had

never bothered to equip the local teachers with the necessary skills and knowledge. To add to

the problem, the country had multiple language groups making communication unwieldy

and irksome.

There is cynicism about the native leadership, too. Roly Dando represents the

cynical view about the independent country's future. According to him, the new native

leaders will eventually become corrupt. Ania Loomba says that 'Colonialism' is not just something that happens from outside a country or people, not just something that operates with the collusion of forces from inside, "but a version of it can be duplicated from within. So that 'postcolonialism', far from being a term that can be indiscriminately applied, appears to be riddled with contradictions and qualifications" (16).

This postcolonial scenario is replicated in this Central African country also. Roly Dando says," They're still at the dedicated, puritanical stage, in the government–first'll come the bribery and the purges, then'll come the normal drinking in pubs, along with ordinary mortals like ourselves. They'll settle down" (Guest 49). Postcolonial ills will slowly stalk the country one by one. Shinza also quotes from Fanon who has said that one should be able to cry, "Stop thief!" to whoever the thief is. Fanon has said that while the natives fight for independence there is a clear demarcation between good and evil. However, after getting independence, there are exploiters even among blacks.

> . . . yet everything seemed to be so simple before: bad people were on one side, and the good on the other. The clear, the unreal, the idyllic light of the beginning is followed by a semi-darkness that bewilders the senses. The people find out that the iniquitous fact of exploitation can wear a black face, or an Arab one; and they raise the cry of 'Treason!" But the cry is mistaken; and the mistake must be corrected. The treason is not national, it is social. The people must be taught to cry 'Stop thief!' In their weary road towards rational knowledge the people must also give up their too-simple conception of their overlords. (Fanon. qtd. in Guest 292)

The Party has lost its integrity that was its stamp during the struggle. The degeneration of the Party is evident in the way it treats its women and peasants. This is a postcolonial marginalization. Another type of colonialism emerges when the party, instead of being a people's party, becomes "a party of cabinet ministers, civil servants and businessmen" (Guest 344). Shinza differentiates the Party's stand before and after independence. "If we were a classless people, we are now creating a dispossessed peasant proletariat of our own. The lives of the people in the rural areas are stagnant. If PIP as a ruling party is to remain a people's party it was through the Independence struggle, it must recognize what it has allowed to happen" (Guest 343).

After independence, there has developed a dichotomy between the workers and the government, whereas before independence, nationalistic spirit was inseparable from the trade unions. Shinza says,

> In our country as in most other African states, before independence
> nationalism was given priority in trade union activities because the economic
> and social situation of the African worker was a direct consequence of
> colonialism. Now that Independence is gained, economic and social
> problems come to the fore again–look at them all around us in the strikes
> and riots, on the mines, the fisheries, the railways. (Guest 360)

Therefore, now, the same conditions prevail as in the days of colonialism. The colonizer need not have a white face; he can have a black face as well.

Shinza's is the voice that discerns the gap between the struggle for independence and the postcolonial struggle for social justice. The Party had always striven for rural uplift.

149

However, in the first Congress of the Party since it formed government, there exist voices asking for elementary rights for farm labourers as a working force. In the seventh Congress since its inception, women's organizations have to protest because they are shut out from Congress. Such voices of dissent are necessary to put the Party in the right path of uniform development of all sections. Shinza regrets that their women who, from the beginning, worked for Independence alongside the men "have been left outside to make tea while Congress debates decisions that will affect their lives and their children's lives" (Guest 343). Independence has not made any difference in the lives of people in the countryside. This fact is brought out when Gordimer says that these people "could feel nearly as remote from what goes on in parliament as they did when it wasn't their government" (Guest 66).

Frantz Fanon's Black Skin, White Masks defines colonized people as those "in whose soul an inferiority complex has been created by the death and burial of its local cultural originality" (18).

A Guest of Honour, while presenting a review of the educational system in an African country, describes this colonial fallout. The African natives have forgotten their own languages and they fumble learning the foreign tongue. English is taught to them in an artificial setting. The linguistic content and the textual context do not tally with their real life. They do no not have any authentic models of speakers with whom they can establish warm rapport that is necessary for language learning. For example, a black teacher who feels inferior in the presence of Bray mentions that he is uncertain about the meaning of the word 'mollify'. Bray, too, pretends to be uncertain about the meaning, because he wants to put the poor teacher at ease. He impulsively pretends "out of civilized courtesy of his kind, that uncertainty about the meaning of the word was something anyone might share–and this in itself was part of the very absurdity: the assumptions of colonial culture"(Guest 80). Bray is self-critical about his colonial mentality.

The colonized people's willingness to be mastered by the British is expressed in many an instance. Blacks, too, were guilty of this complicity in the committing of the crime of imperialism. Many former white sympathizers like Bray got coveted posts in the new government for their role in their freedom struggle. Bray feels guilty about "the disproportionate return he was getting for a commonplace interest" in their lives (Guest 82).

It is typical of a postcolonial country to have different mentalities among whites. While some whites are content to play a role in a new black democracy, others have gone back to their country. Yet another group stayed on because of the nature of their business despite their colonial feelings. Such whites express their displeasure and resentment at the aspirations of blacks. Gordimer says that in Africa, whites were divided into two groups: both groups would not have come together in colonial times because one group viewed Africans as the owners of their country, and the other group viewed them "as a race of servants with good masters" (Guest 192).

Mrs. Pilchey is a typical white who believes that white colonizers were the redeemers of blacks who were very backward and who needed civilization and chastising at the hands of whites. Mrs. Pilchey who runs hotel business spits venom when she derogatorily remarks on the dreams of her kitchen boys. "You can't get anybody to do anything. *They* don't care. They want to be rich. They want to fly aeroplanes. That's what I get told by one of my kitchen boys, yes, I'm not telling a lie. He doesn't want to scrub the tables, he wants go to town and learn to fly an aeroplane now" (Guest 82). Her selfish motive of finding suitable kitchen boys is thwarted and hence this contempt for their rightful ambitions.

Postcolonial ills are seen as the inevitable sequel to colonial evils. Bray feels, "A profound cycle of change was set up here three or four hundred years ago, with the first of us foreign invaders. We incline to think it comes to a stop, full circle, with independence . . . but that's not so . . . it's still in process–that's all" (Guest 210).

Bray is not certain whether these remaining ills will be spewed out once and for all, or ingested. He happens to meet the two unmarried sisters, the Misses Fowler, who had been living in this country. Post-independence, they do not want to remain here. Their outlook has changed. "The old girls hadn't wanted to sit in their drawing rooms with Africans, but now they did not set to be left in peace there. They had recognized themselves for an anachronism" (Guest 214).

Colonialism and capitalism go hand in hand. The more an independent country becomes socialist, the more descendents of the invaders would leave the country. "So far, the states that go socialist become the most exclusively African, the capitalist ones have as many or nearly as many descendents of the invaders as before. Not surprising. But, it can alter . . ." (Guest 210).

Bray has shed all vestiges of colonialism; yet he cannot help sympathizing with Mrs. Pilchey when she resents that the Labour laws of the independent country are to her disadvantage. She wants the same colonial powers she had exercised before to retain or sack her employees. She laments that now she cannot oust her kitchen boys without asking the Ministry of Labour first. This reveals how the black boys went unprotected before. Bray could say to her, "I can sympathize; it must be hellish difficult for you" (Guest 83). Mrs. Pilchey accuses Bray and his kind for siding with blacks. "She didn't believe him; it was all very well for people like him who hadn't had to make a living, who were sent out by the British government for a few years and took sides with the blacks because they didn't have to stay and live with them if they didn't want to" (Guest 83). Bray and his kind were neutral in their attitude and, therefore, fellow whites did not appreciate them.

Bray is a humanist who can identify with his fellow whites. He is above petty prejudices and racial hatred. Ten years before, as District Commissioner of Gala, Bray had incurred the wrath of the colonizers who had sent him back to England. Even now, Bray could see the old prejudice in the greetings of the white tradespeople. When Mrs. Pilchey gives up her disgruntled manner and lights up for a while, he is relieved. "He was touched, as always, by a sign of life; but even in the odd moment of warmth she kept in her face an aggression of pride and inferiority: not that *he* and his kind had deigned, had known how to enjoy themselves!"(Guest 84). However, Bray has a sense of history that allows him to see his own doings and others' as forced by the circumstances.

He had no particular awareness of his "position" among them; the past in relation to Mweta and Edward Shinza and the country's future meant

> something to him, but the past in relation to his difficulties in the
> Colonial Service and the settlers was simply an outdated conflict in
> which each side had acted–fair enough–according to the convictions
> in a particular historical situation, a situation that no longer existed.
> (Guest 92)

Bray's love is universal; he embraces the whole humanity. He accepts the colonial past as necessitated by history. His anti-colonial stand was precipitated by the historical situation. The hate-campaign he faced from some colonizers is not relevant now.

Hjalmar Wentz also shares Bray's unprejudiced attitude towards the black people. White supremacists tend to think that drunkenness and violence belong to the so-called inferior races. When there is a discussion about the high incidence of rail accidents in the independent country, the white men blame the black engine drivers immediately. African drivers are accused of drinking heavily while on duty. Hjalmar Wentz does not differentiate between blacks and whites in this regard. According to him, these are all assumptions and misunderstandings about blacks. Wentz sees beyond these prejudices and perceives the truth.

> Of course, they are drinking. They have to show somehow to themselves that
> the new life is good, how do these whites think their great-grandfathers
> behaved when they first got wages for a week's work in a factory in
> Europe, eh? These Englishmen–their great-grandfathers were getting
> drunk on cheap gin, and they turn up their noses at the Africans.
> (Guest 150)

He also expresses the hope that soon Mweta's government will make it an offence to drink before one goes for duty. The country will tide over the initial hiccups and the men will soon learn to impose a code of behaviour.

Gordimer does the job of writing back to the empire when she points out the ills shared by all the people, irrespective of the colour of the skin. The author talks about a black woman called Mary Odise who "trained as a social worker in Birmingham, where she had investigated the wife-beating, child neglect and drunkenness of the people who had brought white civilization to her country"(Guest 189). Odise told him that once a white woman told her, after pouring out all her sordid tale, that she did not feel ashamed with her as she was a 'blackie'.

Bray is sincere in feeling happiness for the independence of the country when he attends a dinner party hosted by the President. The authorial voice recalls decades of servitude of the blacks and its painful memories, when she describes the applause of the black audience for the performance of their black leader. Their president Mweta, along with his wife, entertains the audience. "The Africans merely looked indulgent; after forty years of being told when to come and go, when to stand and when to take your hat off, a black president himself decided upon procedure"(Guest 196).

James Bray, a white man, had had a meaningful role in the colonial past. He had supported blacks' liberation movement. He believed that by opposing colonialism while being a part of it was something that was necessary for allowing the independence inside.

I understood perfectly what I was doing. . . . When Shinza and Mweta started PIP, it was something I believed in. The apparent contradiction between my position as a colonial servant and this belief wasn't really a contradiction at all, because to me it was the contradiction in the colonial system–the contradiction that was the live thing in it, dialectically speaking, its transcendent element, that would split it open by identifying it, and let the future out–the future of colonialism *was* its own overthrow and the emergence of Africans into their own responsibility. (Guest 247)

However, the resolution is not complete. Economic colonization continues. Shinza is critical about Mweta's foreign policy.

According to Shinza, the dialectic between trade unionism and foreign capital will spiral into a positive result–defending the country's natural resources. Opposition to the government should be viewed as a constructive step, since it will help the government to reach the people. Shinza holds the view that after independence, trade unionism is the population's means of defence against foreign capital. Getting the active involvement of the independent trade union opinion in matters of foreign capital investment is more important than the rubber stamp of a government appointee.

Bray has genuine concern for the state of education in the country. He is aware of the irrelevance of English education in Africa. The English administrators had modelled African education on European education system. Therefore, the child was never familiar with the cultural context of what was being taught.

What was needed was perhaps someone with knowledge of the latest basic
techniques of learning. Someone who could cut through the old assumptions
that relied so heavily on a particular cultural background, and concentrate
on the learning process itself. That should be freed to form its own
correlation to a relevant culture. (Guest 101)

Bray thinks it is preposterous to ask an African student "to write a letter to a friend
describing a trip abroad with your aunt" (Guest 101). This simple example of the
imposition of the British system of education on the local population without considering
their needs is typical of the colonial domination.

The challenges before the independent country make Bray realize the colonial
failures. Gordimer describes Bray's visit to a fishmeal factory and an adjoining village.

Naked children and scavenging dogs were about; then he noticed that a
series of derelict sheds under the rotting tin roof were not storage sheds at
all, although they stank like them, but were inhabited. There were no
windows, only the dark holes of doorways. Faces loomed in the darkness;
now he saw that what he had taken for rubbish lying about were the
household possessions of these people. (Guest 232)

The state of the huts and the conditions of inmates put him into shame. "He felt ashamed
to walk up and stare at the people but he walked rapidly past, a few feet away, in the peculiar
awe that the sight of acquiescent degradation produces in the well-fed" (Guest 232).

Thus, the novel <u>A Guest of Honour</u> lends itself to a study from a postcolonial perspective because the writer has recorded the events that could possibly take place in a newly independent nation. Issues like poverty, corruption, power struggles within parties and the continuing dependence on the former colonizer are common in new democracies.

Unlike the typical postcolonial writers who racially belong to the former colonies, Gordimer is ethnically European and writes in a European language. A question of whether one can read her as if she were a native writer, arises. It is appropriate and relevant to read her from a postcolonial perspective because her loyalties, both as a novelist and as an activist, were not with the rulers. Postcolonial approach does justice to her literary texts, because she is a spokesperson of the oppressed people, without misgivings or prejudice. She wrote against the policies of the rulers in the hope that constructive criticism will address problems of immediate human concern.

The next chapter analyses the stylistic aspects of Gordimer's novels. Since form and content are two sides of the same coin, an in-depth study of style yields more insights into her content.

Chapter-V

Fastidiousness and Erudition: the Hallmarks of Gordimer's Craft

Tell me,

What's poetic

about shooting defenceless kids

in a Soweto street?

Can there be poetry

in fostering Plural Relations?

Can there be poetry

in the Immorality Act?

What's poetic

about deciding other people's lives?

. . . .

As long as

this land, my country

is unpoetic in its doings

it'll be poetic to disagree.

(Gwala. qtd. in Walder 170)

Style in literary parlance means the way a writer chooses to treat his or her subject or theme. In other words, subject dictates style. Secondly, style decides the readership or audience for a particular author. Therefore, a writer determines the method of treatment of his or her subject keeping the specific theme and the target audience in mind.

159

Style coincides with the author's unconscious intention, which is realized in his or her fiction. Lukács says style "is rooted in content; style is the specific form of a specific content. Content determines form" (476). Literature depicting difficult times may be narrow in its range of themes; but the interest it creates and the power it wields are great enough to cause revolution and change. Dennis Walder suggests that literature written under stressful social and political circumstances may be symptomatic of the end of such tyrannical circumstances. Walder writes, "Literature under these circumstances seems symptomatic: of the end of colonialism, and the beginning of a new era; which is what gives such literature its interest, and power, although it also suggests its potential narrowness" (152).

Most of Gordimer's works were unread by black African readers because they were too complex. That was one of the reasons for the South African Government not banning some of her works. Those in the government were well aware that the common South African black reader was unlikely to be influenced by Gordimer's works because she was out of his grasp. The novels of Gordimer escaped ban with a few exceptions because the government considered her writing too urbane for most South African readers to comprehend them. Dennis Walder says, "Within South Africa, where her works have been almost as often banned as praised, recognition has been much slower in arriving, and even now appears grudging" (159).

Political and social imbalances put the native readers at a disadvantageous position. Gordimer wrote in support of the underprivileged, yet the underprivileged masses had no means of accessing her books.

Gordimer is read by and large by an overseas and local white elite
(somewhat of a contradiction, since her work has remained caught into the
system of privilege and the confinements of the present, which her writing
has protested against), partly because these are the audiences who have
had access to her work as a result of the imbalances apartheid has caused
and partly because of the tradition, and the complex literary fretwork,
within which she writes. (Nuttall 13)

Dorothy Driver writes that her kind of sophisticated writing was not for lay audience.
The African "censors continued to ban 'populist' writing said to be designed to provoke
racial hatred or to lead to social unrest, but permitted oppositional texts unlikely to have
mass appeal"(Driver 100). No local publishers were willing to promote works that had no
mass appeal.

SA authodic
r
Censorship

Gordimer's publishers were either British or American. The critic further states,
"Local publishers continually struggle to make ends meet . . . most South African fiction
is published in Britain and then distributed in South Africa; thus, neither the best sellers
nor the slower but dependable sellers (J. M. Coetzee, Nadine Gordimer and
Andre Brink) are in fact local commodities" (100).

A remarkable fact about Gordimer's books is that reading them requires continuous
intellectual exercise on the part of the reader. The pleasure or joy of reading her books
lies in labouring through her prose and grasping the stated and unstated sense of her
words. Even the most patient reader is plagued continually by doubt about his or her

Engaging
Readers
intellect

161

comprehension of <u>The Conservationist</u> or <u>Burger's Daughter</u>. Critics have felt that her works demand that the reader be highly literate and literary. In other words, many of her works are too erudite to be comprehended fully. Nuttall says,

> Gordimer's own world and world of her fiction have been highly 'mediated' by her reading although she also always includes those other areas of her life, like sexuality, which involved the encounter with "otherness" and contributed to her growth as a writer. Similarly, too literary a reading of Gordimer's work would be a distortion of it, but Gordimer's extensive use of literary signifiers and the intertextual quality of her work nevertheless imply a highly literate and literary reader. (13)

The complexity of her prose springs from her scholarship and her toeing the line of European authors. The flesh and blood of her writing is South African but the garb is European. Therefore, in spite of openly espousing the cause of liberation movement and other native cultural bodies, she is inaccessible to native readers because she remains Eurocentric as far as her style is concerned. Her English is exclusively European, not much tinted by local colourings. Dennis Walder accedes, "Gordimer's work can be said to represent . . . the historically dominant, elitist English tradition, validated by external, metropolitan cultural media" (159).

The most notable feature of her style is her controlled and distant tone. The author is almost clinical in her approach to her themes and characters. There are contorted and convoluted expressions and very lengthy interior monologues with characters that are not

162

present before the speakers. Syntax is altered; semantics is in a flux. In other words, the author explores all linguistic possibilities to suit her purpose. The writer's linguistic and stylistic preferences set her works apart from populist fiction.

The South African subject did not allow Gordimer to choose an easy and intimate style. In addition to being a great reader and scholar in world literature, she is a keen observer of political events across the world. She has a lucid comprehension of philosophies like Marxism and Existentialism. Her scholarship in German, French, and contemporary African literatures is amazing. Her rich apperceptive mass facilitated a thorough scholarly approach to her themes.

This chapter seeks to probe whether her subject dictated her style. The chapter also attempts to capture the essential Gordimer. In addition, it focuses on historicity and intertexts in her works.

Many critics have pointed out the fact that Gordimer's novels depict so much of South African history that some of them read like documentaries. In fact, novel and history seem to have merged into one in some of her works. Susan Gallagher has quoted from J. M. Coetzee's speech "The Novel Today" in her essay titled "The Backward Glance: History and the Novel in Post-apartheid South Africa." In this speech delivered in 1987, Coetzee commented that novel has been colonized by history. Coetzee also feared that the South African novel, under the powerful influence of apartheid, seemed to be subsumed by history. He has mentioned that a novelist who failed to investigate real historical circumstances would be considered as lacking in seriousness. According to Coetzee, novels written "in times of intense ideological pressure like the present" tend to have the quality of either "supplementarity" or "rivalry" (qtd. in Gallagher 377). He also adds that if a novel is documentary or reportorial of the current political events then it is said to have supplementarity. This quality provides a vicarious experience to the reader of being present in the political scene. On the other hand, the novel as rival is one that "operates in terms of its procedures   and issues in its own conclusions, not one that operates in terms of the procedures of history and eventuates in conclusions that are checkable by history . . ." (qtd. in Gallagher 378). He further stated that the novel as rival "evolves its own paradigms and myths, in the process . . . perhaps going so far as to show up in mythic status of history"(qtd. in Gallagher 378).

A novelist looks at universal truths and makes predictions based on those truths. Gordimer created her own forecasts and projections about the future of South Africa. She has suggested the future destruction of apartheid through revolutionary means in July's People and A Sport of Nature. These novels are seen as anticipatory ones given the conditions that prevailed in South Africa at that time.

However, the path to the end of apartheid had not been as brutal as it has been predicted. Gordimer attributes the reason for the smooth transition of power to Mandela's wisdom and magnanimity.

In this connection it is relevant to recall what T. S. Eliot means by the phrase 'the historical sense'. He says,

> . . . the historical sense involves a perception, not only of the pastness
> of the past, but of its presence; the historical sense compels a man to

write not merely with his own generation in his bones, but with a

feeling that the whole of the literature of Europe from Homer and

within it the whole of the literature of his own country has a

simultaneous existence and composes a simultaneous order. (72)

Gordimer's grasp of the world literature is similar to her grasp of the world affairs.

She does not see South Africa as an isolated instance. She locates South Africa in the

universal scheme of things. This enables her to see suffering as a continuum.

Gordimer's works do not stop with providing a first-hand experience of South African

history; they provide universal dimensions to local problems. Her novels do not merely

present verifiable, authentic facts; they present perpetual facets of truth.

Dennis Brutus, another critic of Gordimer, has suggested, "The dehumanization and

coldness of apartheid has penetrated her very style" (97). According to him, she "lacks

warmth, lacks feeling, but can observe with a detachment, with the coldness of a

machine" (97). Critics have also labelled her works as protest literature. Some critics also

wondered in the early 1990s as to what she would write about once apartheid was lifted.

Gordimer seems cold and detached in her style. As Dennis Brutus himself has

suggested, the troubled times might have been responsible for her extraordinarily wry

and humourless prose. However, at least two of her novels show signs of liveliness and

cheerfulness. They are The Pickup and A Sport of Nature. The former is different from

her usual reflective prose because the novel is set partly in the post-apartheid South

Africa and partly in an Arabian country. A Sport of Nature has a cheerful and fun-loving protagonist in Hillela in spite of active participation in political events. Therefore, it can be concluded that she deliberately chose to write in a ponderous style because her subject matter dictated her manner of writing.

In addition to the historicity, the author quite often refers to different philosophers, political ideologues and great thinkers like Solzhenitsyn, Marx, Khrushchev, Mao, Glucksmann, Machiavelli, Des Cartes, Fanon, and many others. This aspect reveals how intimately Gordimer has known different political philosophies. For example, she quotes from Claude Levi-Strauss in the epigraph of <u>Burger's Daughter</u>: "I am the place in which something has occurred." She quotes Marcel Proust and Basho, a seventeenth century Japanese poet. She quotes often from black writers, too.

Gordimer' span of knowledge is so vast that one local incident triggers in her mind a train of thoughts encompassing in one sweep the history of global politics and universal sufferings. For example, <u>Burger's Daughter</u> universalizes the motive behind infliction of suffering and the nature of suffering. Though the inescapable and all-pervading apartheid is her forte, the universalization of the local situation has endeared her to those readers who have humanitarian concerns.

She is a scholarly novelist whom a reader can appreciate better if he or she is equipped with adequate knowledge of political and philosophical treatises of great thinkers. Though she has written <u>A Guest of Honour</u> in the tradition of nineteenth century realism, she has dwelt at length on several political ideologies. The novel follows a comparatively simpler and more direct narrative style. Robert Green says, "The richness of <u>A Guest of Honour</u> is not confined to surface and externals; it is also a wonderfully intelligent rendering of political theories and ideologies, revealing on every page Gordimer's recent immersion in Nkrumah, Cabral, Nyerere and Fanon, without ever jeopardizing its narrative magnetism" (554). The novel finely balances narration and discussion of political ideologies.

Post-apartheid, her novels prove that she has transcended the narrow confines of *Post - apartheid* the apartheid themes. In spite of her repetitive themes and locale, her aim is not simply to be politically exact. Her objective as a responsible artist has been to develop a new consciousness among the readers. She has succeeded in fulfilling the task of a committed writer in troubled times. What Gordimer says about art is true about her own works: ". . . events change to consciousness of the world, it shakes and the shocks register seismographically in movements in art" (Burger 291).

Her works have also registered the social and political upheavals of her times. It is natural not to write about apartheid once the conditions change. Gordimer's latest novel The Pickup is evidence that she has already moved beyond the shores of apartheid, because this novel explores the hitherto unexplored regions both geographically and thematically.

Gordimer's earlier works are straight narratives in the realistic tradition. They follow the narrative patterns suitable to social realism whereas her later novels are not straight or linear narratives. Beginning with The Conservationist, she has followed a modernist narrative method. The narrative goes back and forth in time. The point of view changes from that of a character to that of the author. This style is suitable to reflective themes as in The Conservationist, and Burger's Daughter. There is not much action in both the novels. She has employed the stream of consciousness technique along with the authorial point of view. The protagonists or the speakers in these novels speak a lot with other characters who are not present before them. These protagonists are very intelligent and capable of holding lengthy dialogues in their minds. Rosa's dialogue with Conrad in absentia runs to more than six pages:

> To be free is to become almost a stranger to oneself: the nearest I'll ever
> get to see what they saw outside the prison. If I could have seen that,
> I could have seen that other father, the stranger to myself. I seem always to
> have known of his existence.

> I suppose you found another place to live. (Mexico perhaps.) We didn't
> bump into each other around town. (You never knew about the man in the
> park). But you were the one who had said–why'd you talk about him as
> 'Lionel' . . . the bloodshot eyes that could not look at him whom she had
> betrayed. (Burger 81-87)

The listener is absent and this fact is revealed by her own words in the style of dramatic monologue. Yet, the conversation differs from dramatic monologue. In dramatic monologue, the listener is present, whereas Rosa holds the dialogue in her head and anticipates the possible questions her listener may be curious to ask.

The long dialogues are actually attempts at resolution of dialectic in the character's mind. That is why the author chooses to make the characters speak in their minds. The actual dialogue cannot be manipulated because the listener may be autonomous in his replies.

The direction of the dialogue will be determined by the actual listener's response. Only if the listener is not present, could the speaker resolve her conflict. The speaker dictates the conversation because the problem is inside her head. Rosa herself guesses the train of thoughts in Conrad's mind. It is the speaker's unique problem, which only she could resolve.

The central character in Burger's Daughter is too young to view the world history or ideologies. Therefore, the author's point of view is necessary to portray a convincing discussion. In other words, the author speaks the words that Rosa might not have spoken. This is the reason why the authorial intervention is used.

My Son's Story is narrated by the authorial voice as well as by Will. The reason for making the son a partial narrator is to make the story sound immediate and convincing. The experiences become authentic once a character who had been a witness becomes the narrator. John E. Tilford says, "One of the basic functions of fiction, paradoxically, is to sound true. The point of view from which the story is told has much to do with verisimilitude. . . . The quickest way to achieve verisimilitude . . . is to let a witness tell the story" (289).

My Son's Story has more action than The Conservationist because there are incidents that cause turning points in this novel. The author intervenes to present the characters as seen from different angles or to describe scenes in which the characters are not present. For example, Will is not present in the scenes where his father and Hannah are present. In addition to being inaccessible, Sonny and Hannah indulge in an act of betrayal, which is supposed to be a secret. According to Tilford, "the narrator can only report what he says and does and what he hears and sees others saying and doing" (290). The authorial voice helps narrating the love life of Sonny and Hannah, which happens in the absence of Will in My Son's Story. Will is an adolescent boy and, therefore, he is barred from describing the private life of his father. Using Will in other contexts helps the author portray the emotional handicap caused to the family by the betrayal of Sonny who is the protagonist. Gordimer uses Will's voice, in addition to the authorial voice, because there are several advantages of using such a character. To quote Tilford again,

> . . . the story is told by somebody inside it, with resultant verisimilitude. Moreover, the narrator-participant-witness provides a consistent, compelling focus for the action; and his commentary and evaluation from his point of view allow him to serve as a kind of guide to the reader. Finally, this method may add to the complexity of the story and increase its possibilities for richness. (292)

Narrative voice

The Conservationist is yet another novel in which the central character's stream of consciousness is interrupted by the author. The narrative mode is very complex in the novel. The author intervenes here for two obvious purposes: first, to narrate what happens on the farm during Mehring's long absence; second, to describe the farm during drought and rains. In addition, the author intervenes to introduce the family of De Beers, the Indians and, of course, Mehring himself.

The author intervenes to speak about the weather change. Some of the descriptions are too poetical to make the pig-iron dealer speak them. For instance, the author pictures the cyclone and heavy rains battering the farm: "The weather came from the Mozambique

Channel. Space is conceived as trackless but there are beats about the world frequented by cyclones given female names. One of these beats crosses the Indian Ocean by way of the islands of Seychelles, Madagascar, and the Mascarenes" (Conser. 232). The description ranges from far to near when she depicts the devastating effects of a cyclone.

> A cyclone paused somewhere miles out to sea, miles up in the atmosphere, its vast hesitation raising a draught of tidal waves, wavering first towards one side of the island, then over the mountains to the other, darkening the thousand up-turned mirrors of the rice paddies and finally taking off again with a sweep that shed, monstrous cosmic peacock, gross paillettes of hail, a dross of battering rain and all the smashed flying detritus of uprooted trees, tin roofs and dead beasts caught up in it. (Conser. 232)

Gordimer, thus, attempts to capture the cosmic drama of the cyclone in words. The power of the rain is also a symbol for the revolution and uprising. The rain is so powerful that the slamming ropes of rain have ploughed up the soil exposing the shallowly buried dead body of the black man. The sun appears unwillingly after three days of rain: "On the Friday the sky held for a few hours and there was a tender area of glare where the sun must have been buried, a grey pearl in jeweller's cotton wool or an opaque insect-egg swathed in web . . ." (Conser. 234).

Gordimer's exclusive style is suitable to narrate stories about white intellectual characters. Her elite narrative style is too complicated to write about the hapless non-intellectual characters. As has been pointed out by critics, Gordimer has preferred a sophisticated style to lend voice to the humble blacks. Definitely, her style makes a statement that the urbane readers should revise their outlook of the situation prevailing in South Africa. Her style also shows that Gordimer did not make any pretensions about her attitude towards blacks. She has written in a manner that comes easily to her. Only such a style would rightly convey the role of whites in the drama of apartheid. Her target readers were the privileged; her point of view was that of a white. Gordimer has made it known that she could never comprehend what it means to be a black. So, she seldom ventures into a black character's mind. Human psychology is within the grasp of the author; blacks' psychology is subsumed under human psychology. Therefore, the author could easily empathize with blacks.

South Africa is the locale of Gordimer's major works. She has also written novels situated in countries bordering South Africa but the main scene of action is South Africa. Sometimes, her characters have relatives living in England or other European countries. For instance, half of the action in Burger's Daughter happens in Europe. She has also written novels about imaginary countries as in A Guest of Honour and The Sport of Nature. The Pickup begins in South Africa, but soon the scene shifts to an unnamed Arab country. However, it is not often that she moves away from her home country. Whatever the locale, Gordimer used it as a canvass to paint life and truth.

Novel is an imaginary medium, yet the author speaks the undeniable truth about the place. She wrote at a time when the well-meaning world looked at apartheid with loathing. She wrote when the United Nations and the developed countries imposed sanctions on South Africa. She wrote when humanitarian values were at an all time low; she wrote at a time when works in support of the blacks' cause were being banned.

She wrote when the outside world had no means of knowing about the atrocities taking place in South Africa. When the world did not understand the pain in the Dark Continent, her works bore the torch in whose light the world understood the struggle that was ripping South Africa for over half a century. Her works helped the world to understand South Africa, which was not allowed even to play international cricket until the curtain fell on apartheid.

Gordimer's art brought about a sympathetic understanding of the other. People of a particular country appreciate the rest of the world best through art; art succeeds when all else fails. Art covers the common ground among people of different countries; therefore, art paves the way for mutual understanding. Eudora Welty says, "Mutual understanding in the world being nearly always, as now, at low ebb it is comforting to remember that it is through art that one country can nearly always speak reliably to another, if the other can hear at all" (232). Fiction, ironically, becomes a way of recording the truth about a place.

There is no single self-contained literary critical theory that can help analyze the entire gamut of literary genres and themes. There have been different literary critical theories and approaches that have tried to explain literary creations. Some of the theories have been more convincing than the others in their ability to analyze the methods and techniques used by writers. However, no single theory has been free from fallacies that come attached as tags to theories. For example, the theory of New Criticism caused great waves when it first appeared. The New Critical theory suggested that a literary work is meaningful in itself and a reader has no need to seek outside information for a full

[handwritten annotation: New criticism — Stand alone]

comprehension and appreciation of a text. However, one will definitely agree that at least some literary works can be better appreciated if the historical or biographical factors of the author are taken into account. Akin to the case of New Criticism, almost all critical theories suffer from one fallacy or the other.

Nevertheless, most critics would agree that any new literary work is the sum total of the experiences, readings and thoughts of the writers. No writer is free from the past and present, political and social influences of the place where he was born or the place where he lives. No text is a separate entity without the influence and confluence of the previous writings and happenings. All individual talent is tinted by history or tradition.

Similarly, there is no reader without a background. Every reader approaches a text with the schema that has already been formed in his mind by what he has read, seen, heard and experienced. An individual is the sum total of what he has read, seen, heard, and experienced. His comprehension and appreciation of a text depends on the richness of the prearranged schema. In other words, the text does not exist until a reader reads it. The reader brings meaning to the text. Every text is informed by the other texts that the reader has read and the reader's own cultural context. The more informed a reader is, the more meaningful the text becomes.

Art is not free from the contemporary social and political happenings for the same reason that the artist is not free from them. In addition, art is not free from the other art forms. A film is made under the influence of the other contemporary films and the films before it. Likewise, the themes and techniques employed in other art forms are also determined by the events and happenings of the milieu in which the creative artist lives.

It is in this light that intertextuality becomes a more meaningful and convincing theory. The term intertextualty is often mistakenly used to mean the way texts intersect. But, by this term, Julia Kristeva "meant *the passage from one sign system to another*– the way in which one signifying practice is transposed into another" (qtd. in McAfee 26).

The following are the basic assumptions of intertextuality:

- A literary piece is the result of its relationship to other texts and to structures of language itself.
- Other literary and extra-literary materials have a great role to play in the making of a work of literature.
- All literary production takes place in the presence of other texts.
- Only a reader brings meaning to a text.
- Sometimes, apart from other literary works, historical and social factors also determine the literary practices of writers.

Julia Kristeva, the Bulgarian critic and philosopher, introduced the semiotic theory of intertextuality. She referred to texts in terms of two axes: a horizontal axis connecting the author and reader of a text, and the vertical axis, which connects the text to other texts. Uniting these two texts are shared codes. Every text and every reading depends on prior codes. Kristeva declared that every text is under the control of other discourses, which impose a universe on it. She argued that a text is not an independent entity. Therefore, instead of looking at its structure, one should look at its structuration (how the structure came into being). This involves studying the text within the totality of previous or synchronic texts of which the present text is a "transformation."

175

Intertexuality is something far more than the influences of writers on each other. It is derived from the Latin word "intertext," meaning to intermingle while weaving. Julia Kristeva departs from the tradition of referring to an author's "influences" and the text's sources. Instead, she claims that all signifying systems are constituted by the manner in which they transform earlier signifying systems. A literary work is not simply the product of a single author, but of its relationship to other texts, and to the structures of language itself. She emphasized that any text is constructed of a mosaic of quotations; any text is the absorption and transformation of another.

Intertextuality is a new way of accounting for the role of literary and extra-literary materials without resorting to traditional ideas of authorship. There has been language and literature before and around the text. Knowingly or unknowingly, different texts are placed within the text. Intertexts need not be simply "literary"; historical and social determinants themselves are meaningful texts that transform and modify literary practices. Political scenario becomes a part of history. Political situations of intensive character tend to make writers out of ideologists. Oppressive political climate makes authors cringe in fear. When a book is banned or when a fellow-writer faces incriminating charges, some writers think of skirting the burning issues. Sometimes, when creative writings are banned, aggressive feelings are fanned and writers choose to write more about the burning issues. Much of what one faces in reality is found in books, newspapers, magazines, and other media. These are called intertexts.

Such writings influence the opinion of the world community. Reality is affected by texts as much as texts are affected by reality. Intertextuality blurs the boundaries between texts and reality. Artists reflect reality and reality in turn is transformed by art. In this sense, great artists have caused great awakenings. Gordimer can be said to have interwoven historical and social intertexts into her novels in order to create an awakening in her readers. She used political and social intertexts in her fiction to mobilize world opinion against apartheid.

Sarah Nuttall, who has analyzed both black and white writers' texts, concludes that generally white women's texts are more literary than most black women's, revealing the specialty of the tradition they are written in. "The texts refer frequently to other texts within their own, employing an intertextuality generally not found in black women's writing" (Nuttall 12). Again she says, "Reading experiences often signal significant movements in characters' lives, a feature which derives as much from a writer like Virginia Woolf as it does from other white South African women writers many of whom use books to signal escape from a repressive, colonial context" (12).

There is a charge that Gordimer's texts are stereotypes. She was blamed for not writing about the real people. As writers are sensitive and sharp, they cannot but write about the political and social turmoil surrounding them. In fact, such harsh atmosphere will inform most of their writings. Even when the outside climate is oppressive, the domestic and interpersonal woes are not negligible. However, the primary theme in the minds of democratic-minded writers would be to reflect the political and social climate rather than the interpersonal relationships and the conflicts in the domestic front. When the question of peaceful existence itself is a more pressing issue, domestic dilemmas and conflicts become mere squabbles not worth taking notice.

Racial discrimination touched upon the lives of the people so much so that even personal relationships were linked to the inhuman national scenario. No text of Gordimer's is free from this scenario because no individual is free from the influences of the inhospitable circumstances. No sensitive writer is free from this adverse climate. For example, whenever there were great movements and revolutions, writers wrote about them. When India was partitioned, novels spoke about the wounds and gashes caused by the ripping apart of the nation. This is because the magnitude of such an event is all embracing and all pervading. As the wounds heal, writers turn to more mundane and more interpersonal themes. It is natural that when there is a great calamity, or when there is no respect for human life or values, an individual's unique problem is not worth dealing with. That was what happened during the Holocaust and the genocide in Germany. These incidents pervade all art forms and they determine the texts of many writers who lived in that era. Human relationships are relegated to the background and the most significant historical and social happenings are foregrounded.

Gordimer happened to live in an extraordinary period. By weaving the social and political intertexts into her fiction, the author made the world look up and take notice. By writing about the most pressing question, she proved that the most human question in the world is equity and justice. As a result of the works of her ilk, South Africa was isolated and economic sanctions were slapped against it. This isolation made the South African Government think about withdrawing the apartheid policy and restoring democracy to the people of South Africa during the final decade of the twentieth century.

Black and white African writers could not use the novel as an art medium. Instead, they used the novel form for effecting social and political change. Writers had to have this commitment to have an effect on the world readers. Gordimer was no exception. Her novels have to be read with the South African social and political background in mind. The following are some of the social and political intertexts interwoven into her works.

- A large majority of people were denied education: they were cut off from modern cultural influences such as art galleries, libraries, theatres and concerts. In short, they lived in a sort of cultural vacuum.
- Four fifths of the workforce was treated as slave labourers.
- The majority of the people were always reminded of their inferior status by separate racial signs on washrooms, restaurants, laundries, trains, buses, theatres and even graveyards.
- The majority of the people were housed in ghettos and shantytowns.
- About twenty five thousand so called political prisoners were rotting away in jails.
- New prohibitory laws were enacted every other day to make the lives of blacks more and more miserable.
- Blacks were constantly on the move. They were displaced in order to remove them from the vicinity of their masters.

These and the other political phenomena find expression in her fiction. Reality is interwoven into the imaginary situations. The reversal of the conditions prevailing in South Africa is portrayed in her futuristic novel, July's People. Master-servant relationship or victimizer-victim relationship is transposed in the novel in order to create a feeling of shock in the minds of the white readers. The real context or reality is reversed with a purpose. The lesson is this: if whites continue to harass blacks, the day will not be far when the victimizers themselves will be at the mercy of the victims. Whites are made to see the preposterous and tragic situation of their dependence on blacks. Here, political and social reality is the intertext used to create an effect. When she reversed the reality outside the text and presented it imaginatively, the world outside South Africa could sense the intensity of the reality in her country. This example is only to give an inkling of the kind of commitment she had as a writer. Writers of her kind have proved repeatedly that art is for life's sake also.

Some of Gordimer's novels fall into the category of the initiation story. Therefore, it is worthwhile considering certain aspects of the initiation story. In his essay, "What is an Initiation Story?," Mordecai Marcus has written exhaustively about the origin and occurrence of this concept in fiction. Initiation story is a concept derived from anthropology. Brooks and Warren first used the term in 1943 in Understanding Fiction to define Hemingway's story, "The Killers". Brooks and Warren have defined initiation as a discovery of evil leading to self-understanding or self-discovery. In anthropology, initiation means the rites of passage from childhood or adolescence to maturity. In certain African communities, these ceremonies are conducted to test the endurance of a novice. In literature, this idea is used to describe a stage in all human life.

Initiation stories are about individuals undergoing certain experiences to become mature. Education plays an important role in an initiation story. Marcus says,

[handwritten margin note: Initiation narrative]

The various critical definitions of the initiation story fall into two groups. The first group describes initiation as passage of the young from ignorance about the external world to some vital knowledge. The second describes initiation as an important self-discovery and a resulting adjustment to life and society. (185)

According to Marcus, there are three types of initiation stories. He sums up that some initiations lead only to the threshold of maturity and understanding but do not definitely cross it. Such stories emphasize the shocking effect of experience, and their protagonists tend to be distinctly young. The second category of initiations takes the protagonist across a threshold of maturity and understanding but leaves him enmeshed in a struggle for certainty. These initiations sometimes involve self-discovery. Thirdly, the most decisive initiations take their protagonists firmly into maturity and understanding; or at least show them decisively embarked toward maturity. These initiations usually centre on self-discovery. "For convenience, I will call these types tentative, uncompleted and decisive initiations" (Marcus 186-187).

Several of Gordimer's novels are about young men and women coming to terms with the world. The protagonists in A World of Strangers, Burger's Daughter and My Son's Story are young people. Though the protagonists of None to Accompany Me and July's People are initiating into self-realization, they are middle-aged women. Toby Hood of A World of Strangers attains maturity and awareness in South Africa.

Gordimer shows that life in South Africa has awakened in him a new awareness without which he would have been ignorant and innocent. When his white typist hands in her resignation after she finds him sharing his room with two black men, he feels a nervous excitement. The new excitement or anger is his education. Life in South Africa educates him; he understands that the behaviour of the white girl has sucked all normality out of the room in which he sat between two non-whites. This just anger is the result of the education for Toby who comes with a liberal attitude. What happens in the room is a sampling of the situation prevailing in South Africa. Had Toby Hood continued to live in England, he would not have reacted in this manner.

Another character whose development is traced from girlhood until womanhood is Rosa Burger who is educated by her family circumstances unconsciously. She is both fascinated and repelled by her father. She understands in the end that it is not necessary to adhere to her father's communist ideals if she had to understand her father. The fact that all her father's ideals boil down to love for the sufferers enlightens her. She realizes through a series of incidents and phenomena that her aim is to alleviate pain wherever it is. She comes of age with that realization. Bassie's charge and his negritude provide her with a steely determination instead of shaking her conviction to fight for a good cause in her country. To conclude, Burger's Daughter traces the initiation of a pupil into politics through a series of experiences.

My Son's Story is another initiation story in the repertoire of Gordimer. Will is an adolescent curious about entering the adult life. Will is bombarded with new knowledge during adolescence: knowledge of his father's adultery, knowledge of his sister's involvement in underground political activities, her marriage to an activist and the knowledge of his mother's arrest. Will has to struggle for adjustment to his new knowledge. His father, in fact, had initiated him into reading English literature. Coupled with this reading, the personal and political experience provided by his father make him a writer. Thus, the novel can be defined as an initiation novel sketching the development of Will as a writer.

Once again, the story A Sport of Nature begins with the life of Hillela who is a mere girl in the beginning of the novel. She comes to terms with life in an African country, which is in the birth pangs of independence. She converts all the negative traits into positive ones by choosing black men to ascend in her life. Hers is a complete self-discovery without any weakness. Gordimer calls her a sport of nature; for she is capable of taking the sort of decisions, about which other white girls cannot even imagine. Hers is sexual initiative. She discovers the power of sex to be a way of ascending the social and political ladder. This new knowledge is the launching pad from which she savours success after success.

Sex ascending social political ladder.

Will's initiative belongs to the first type of stories, which lead only "to the threshold of maturity and understanding but definitely do not cross it. Such stories emphasize the shocking effect of experience, and their protagonists tend to be distinctly young" (Marcus 186). Rosa is an example for the second type of initiation, which will take "the protagonists across a threshold of maturity and understanding but leave them enmeshed in a struggle for certainty. These initiations sometimes involve self-discovery" (Marcus 186). Hillela in A Sport of Nature faces the third type of initiation that carries the protagonists "firmly into maturity and understanding, or at least shows them decisively towards maturity" (Marcus 187).

Readable r
complex

Gordimer has written in remarkably two different styles: one, highly readable, and another, very complex. Robert Green says,

> Formally, <u>A Guest of Honour</u> marks the climax of one stage of Gordimer's career; the most detailed, circumstantial, and traditional of her novels, it will be followed by a trio of novels, <u>The Conservationist</u>, <u>Burger's Daughter</u>, and <u>July's People</u>, alike in their narrative forms, although very different from one another, will demand greater skills in interpretation from their readers. The latter three are inescapably difficult novels that insist on being reread. (553)

Green also says, "Sparse and self-reflexive, <u>The Conservationist</u> is a very different breed of novel from any of her earlier works, inaugurates the beginning of a new phase in Gordimer's career" (556).

Burger's Daughter is a challenging novel to the reader. It makes great demands on the reader's comprehension skills and sensibility. About the intricacy of <u>Burger's Daughter</u>, Stephen Gray says,

> Its circuitry is incredibly complex: one has not only to read, but plough a way through it. The dense, knotted, tangled style compels total involvement, total concentration on the reader's part, as Gordimer lines up areas of experience which, possibly, the reader does not know, cannot have known. Thus, to know <u>Burger's Daughter</u> is to have one's experience of one own land extended. (qtd. in Green 557)

Gray further states that the experience of reading <u>Burger's Daughter</u> is a challenge to the readers: "the challenge of having to reshape and reform our own habits and expectations as readers" (qtd. in Green 557). Green says that the text of <u>Burger's Daughter</u> constantly asserts its own inner divisions and dislocations, its frequent changes in voice and tone. He also adds that her early fiction, down to the <u>Guest of Honour</u>, had remained silent about the processes of its composition, whereas <u>Burger's Daughter</u> flaunts its own style as artefact.

Rosa has inner conversations with several characters. Rosa is also seen from different angles.

> Rosa is the centre of the action, yet much of the action is composed not of external political events, but rather of meditations on those same events by Rosa herself and by several other characters. Rosa, then, is seen from so many angles—some sympathetic, others neutral, one actively hostile—that it is very difficult to choose one of these perspectives and associate it with the novelist's own judgment. Such is the variety of the novel's perspectives that Rosa emerges as a complex character and her situation, too, as fluid and full of contradictions. (Green 558)

Gordimer uses ellipsis quite often. In <u>July's People</u>, Gordimer uses cryptic language making it difficult for the reader. Maureen and July resort to their respective languages without pretences when they stand deprived of their mutual trust and respect. "Combined with an elliptical style the narrative form creates problems for the reader" (Bailey 216).

Her language is highly evocative. The very language is suggestive of the divisive nature of the South African society. For example, without mentioning that July is their servant, the author conjures up the generations of slavery suffered by blacks in the opening lines of July's People. The unbridgeable chasm between blacks and whites is suggested in these lines: "July bent at the door and began that day for them as his kind has always done for their kind" (July 1). The entire history of black drudgery is brought out in the following lines: "The knock on the door. Seven o'clock. In governors' residences, commercial hotel rooms, shift bosses' company bungalows, master bedrooms *en suite*–the tea-tray in black hands smelling of Lifebuoy soap" (July 1).

Gordimer uses action-verbs and concrete nouns to bring about the immediacy of feeling. The Smales family, utterly in disbelief about the consequences of the violent revolution, travels to July's village in the bakkie. The journey is described thus:

> People in delirium rise and sink, rise and sink, in and out of lucidity.
> The swaying, shuddering, thudding, flinging stops and the furniture of life
> falls into place. The vehicle was the fever. Chattering metal and raving
> dance of loose bolts in the smell of the children's car-sick. She rose from
> it for gradually longer and longer intervals. At first what fell into place
> was what was vanished, the past (July 3).

In a matter of four days, the Smales have moved centuries back in time. The recoiling of the white family into primeval life is a revelation of the kind of life their counterparts have always led. The description of the hut is in sharp contrast to the comfortable life led by the Smales back in the city.

She slowly began to inhabit the hut around her, empty except for the iron bed, the children asleep on the vehicle seats–the other objects of the place belonged to another category: nothing but stiff rolled-up cowhide, a hoe on the nail, a small pile of rags and part of a broken Primus stove, left against the wall. The hens and chickens are moving there; but the slight sound she heard did not come from them. There would be mice and rats. Flies wandered the air and found the eyes and mouths of her children, probably still smelling of vomit, dirty, sleeping, safe" (July 4).

On the surface level, these sentences are a description of the hut belonging to July's mother. Nevertheless, at the deeper level these lines are a powerful commentary on the abject conditions under which blacks had been kept all these years when the whites' standard of living had been soaring high.

In her later novels, one finds recurring symbols and images. The Conservationist and July's People are like rich allusions to the plight of whites after blacks take over. The symbol of the "pale freckled eggs" in the possession of the black children in the beginning of the novel suggests that the future of South Africa will be in the hands of the blacks. That is, Gordimer makes the progeny of blacks possess the eggs. Mehring simply could not get rid of the thought of the eggs: "A whole clutch of guinea fowl eggs. Eleven. Soon there will be nothing left. In the country. The continent. The oceans, the sky" (Conser. 11). Mehring behaves like a conserver of nature, yet, he forgets that the white man is the greatest intruder or trespasser. Conserving independent cultures is also important. This is a significant omission of the colonial rule. Apartheid violated the laws of peaceful co-existence of not man and nature, but of man and man. Therefore, it violated the rule of conservation of human nature.

Repetition and tiresome long speeches mark <u>The House Gun</u>. The novel thinly disguises lectures as dialogues. Dialogues cease to look natural when characters dwell at length on education policies and the changing nature of land banks. Fiction is monotonously prosaic without genuine emotion.

To make matters worse, there are no punctuation marks to indicate the identity of the speaker. Dashes are used instead of quotation marks. Characters' names are not mentioned. Sometimes, the authorial comments also intervene to further confuse the reader.

> This extraordinary prose tendency is made the more trying by the fact that what Harald and Claudia say, either in interior monologue or to each other, or what constitute the authorial asides on their behalf, are all rolled into one. None of it is indicated by quotation marks, tenses switch mid-sentence and singulars and plurals crash together in frequent disagreement. Gordimer tells us it 'doesn't matter whose thoughts these were' and she often refers to the couple as 'he/she.' (Tarpido 29)

Gordimer's stories do not spell a definite conclusion. Gordimer has disclosed in an interview with Hermione Lee that ending of stories cannot be decisive because any event will have its own consequences. She has conceded that all writers are telling only part of the human story. There is no conclusion. "In this, all that we write is pieced together. Nobody can explain all that was happening in his or her society or age. Whether we go to Tolstoy or Dostoevsky or Proust, or any of the greats. All you can do is to contribute your bit of insight. You pick up a life and when you have created it, watched it, seen it move this way and that, you put it down there but, it doesn't end there" (Gordimer. int. with Lee 4). This view reminds one of Virginia Woolf who said that she was offering "a slice of life" in her works.

Having analyzed Gordimer's novels in detail, the final chapter sums up the conclusions of the research study.

Chapter - VI

Summing Up

"No race has a monopoly on beauty, or intelligence, or strength, and there
will be a place for all at the rendezvous of victory"

(Cesaire. qtd. in Ashcroft and Ahluwalia 142).

This study of the select novels of Gordimer made so far has led to certain findings
and conclusions. This chapter aims at the final evaluation of Gordimer's contribution to
South African literature at a time characterized by intense trauma and political upheavals.

If colonial experience marked the early part of twentieth century, the latter half of
the century witnessed the postcolonial and neocolonial practices. There are traces of the
colonial experience or even outright racist occurrences even in the self-proclaimed
most-democratic countries.

Gordimer has spent the whole of her life in South Africa, where, from her
childhood, she was a witness to the cruel segregation policy. One unassailable conviction
that she nurtured from the beginning until the end of apartheid was the injustice of
imposing racism.

Gordimer has had the rare distinction of writing against her own loyalties. She has
looked in the eye of her own group and that of the other. Her compassion has embraced both
the groups and, hence, she has fulfilled the task of serving the 'whole of man'.

Gordimer's literary life was devoted to the study of the forces of life. In her Nobel Prize Acceptance speech "Writing and Being," Gordimer says that she has thrown ample light "into the bloody yet beautiful labyrinth of human experience, of being" (2).

Gordimer records the voices of those occupying the margins as well as the centre. Her gift to South Africa was to represent a white conscientious worldview. Her writings were pursuits of truth. In her personal as well as political life, Gordimer has proved to be a friend to her 'comrades in arms'.

The power struggle that created inequalities and injustice to particular groups of people is the single anchored theme that universalizes her works. While depicting the power struggle, she exposes the scars suffered by both the perpetrators as well as the victims. Her outlook is an all-encompassing one espousing all the countries though the locale of most of her works is the African soil.

Gordimer talks about marginalization in terms of not only blacks and whites, but also women and men and the marginalization among whites. There are margins within margins and centres within centres. She delivers the message that racism and subordination operate at several rungs. For example, other whites treat East Europeans as inferior, yet these East-Europeans consider native Africans as less than human. In A Guest of Honour, Margot Wentz talks about blacks in a condescending manner, in spite of the fact hers is a Jewish family that has sought asylum in Africa.

Gordimer's farsightedness and vision undermined the foolhardy confidence of the white people. Gordimer declared in more than one novel, in unambiguous terms, that the majority would rule Africa. This honest approach coupled with her ability to embrace the other, won her the goodwill of the African National Congress.

In spite of her acceptance of rightful ownership of Africa by Africans, Gordimer apprehended throughout that the two major races in South Africa could never understand each other fully. This situation was the result of the efforts of the racist governments to segregate the races at all levels. The cultural vacuum and the repulsion towards the other made writers and individuals keep the other at a distance. She knew that the segregated life provided no opportunity to experience the camaraderie necessary for such an understanding between the two races.

She had felt the opposing forces of attraction and repulsion between the two races. For example, James Bray in A Guest of Honour could appreciate the attitude of both whites and blacks though he fought for the unconditional removal of racial barriers. In A World of Strangers Toby Hood has friends who belong to other races. He feels at home with both black and white friends. In fact, he feels no remorse when his white typist Miss McCann resigns because he entertains black friends at his office. In Burger's Daughter, Rosa and her father know no racial differences.

As a postcolonial writer, Gordimer scores most as an anti-colonial writer. She sympathizes with the colonized. She has helped create an international culture that will work as an instrument in the struggle for political independence. The writer equates apartheid with Hitler's genocide tendencies. When Vera's German friend Otto Aberbanel describes the scenes of violence that he happened to record on film, Vera likens blacks in South Africa to Jews in Germany. Violence is a continuum, according to her. She tells him, "You haven't lived here long enough to know. The Nazis didn't end in the war where your parents died, they were reborn here" (None 68).

Alterity is one postcolonial term Gordimer herself practised as a writer. She could enter the minds of others in order to find out the forces behind life. Some of her characters like Hillela and Bray have the ability to enter the other and comprehend the other.

The author also focuses on the postcolonial notions of miscegenation and hybridity. She perceived changes that would sow the seeds for a more equitable South Africa when stark white and black will give place to other mixed races. Through her, the author seems to support interracial marriages and relationships as a panacea for racist misunderstandings.

Gordimer also exposes the hypocrisy of white liberals. In the innermost recesses of their minds, whites do not acknowledge the equality of blacks, though they outwardly profess their liberal notions. Maureen Smales is a classic example for such whites. The author's works reveal her evolution from a liberal to a believer in radicalism. Liberalism is a concession that blacks do not need; what they need is strengthening of their own hands. They should try to construct their image and not depend on the white man's views of blacks. July's choice to speak in his own language in the end symbolizes the native's way of writing back to the centre.

Evidence
1 of
liberalism
2
radicalism

Gordimer's novels illustrate the fact that the white man could not ignore his burden. Even an apolitical citizen like Mehring is obsessed with the thought that blacks will one day inherit Africa. The white capitalist Mehring's mind is burdened with guilt because he has been amassing wealth at the cost of blacks. By making Jacobus and his people make their own decisions, the author suggests that blacks have reached the stage of looking after their own interests.

This leads one to the well-known axiom that the personal and the political are inextricably intermingled in Gordimer's novels. The study also traces the patterns in which the personal and the political interact in the lives of some characters in her works. The mutual suspicion of people belonging to different races is evident in Gordimer's stories and novels. Ramifications of the apartheid law control even their love life. Sonny is an example for an activist who brings havoc to his personal life through his involvement in politics.

None to Accompany Me illustrates the pain of exile and the trauma of adjusting to the new life after the demolition of the walls of apartheid. Oupa's life in None to Accompany Me is an example of hundreds of ex-prisoners who still experience the agony and duress. He had lost a good portion of his youth in prison. Mpho is a young girl who had lost her mother tongue and native culture in England where she spent her childhood as an exile along with her parents. The social implications of exile are far-reaching and heart-rending in such cases.

Gordimer's novels also reveal how the quiet and domestic role of women is shaken rudely by the political happenings. Many of the women protagonists are activists or at least they have association or liaison with activists. Rosa Burger, Vera Stark, Hillela, Aila, Hannah, Pauline, Antonia and Anna Louw are all women who have active political consciousness.

According to some of her women characters, national and social values far outweigh personal values. They cross borders as far as sexuality is concerned. For Hillela and Vera Stark loyalty and fidelity are secondary because there are more pressing social mores like the unhappy predicament of blacks.

Many of the characters experience the feelings of fear, uncertainty and insecurity. Terror, tension, bloodshed, danger and violence mark their life. Ambivalence is a postcolonial experience one observes in Gordimer's Africa. The mutual attraction as well as repulsion between races is portrayed because that was the observable truth in South Africa.

The author has made use of the reversal of fortunes as an effective way of driving home the point that whites will have to quit their position of the power centre. July's People and The Conservationist convey the message in unequivocal terms that South African natives are the rightful owners of South Africa. Her grasp of the political and historical forces at work in South Africa was so complete that she foresaw the inevitable dismantling of apartheid. This reversal of perspective results in new knowledge; that Africa belongs to Africans. This imaginary reversal of positions–whites being dependent on natives–helps in perceiving truth. The truth is the miserable state of the natives.

Critics have appraised Gordimer's preoccupation with the theme of apartheid. Her single-minded pursuit of the theme of apartheid can be explained as the consequence of life in South Africa. She has lived in the midst of brutality and she has been witnessing man's inhumanity to man—the cruel law of apartheid. This explains why her writings are so full of apartheid-related themes. In "Writing and Being," Gordimer has averred, "The writer's themes and characters inevitably are formed by the pressures and distortions of that society as the life of the fisherman is determined by the power of the sea" (9).

Gordimer's writings span a prolonged period of colonial rule. Though South Africa changed hands during the twentieth century, the predicament of the natives did not improve. Apartheid rule replaced the colonial rule. In fact, there was a second innings of the colonial era in the form of apartheid.

Any country's history is shaped by opposing forces. South African history is no exception. Gordimer's works record the changing history of the opposition. The dialectic or the opposing trends of the British and the Afrikaner politics gave way to the conflict involving the black and white races. After the abolition of apartheid, the native rulers are not without problems. The native opposition parties are fighting the native government, thus mimicking the previous dialectic.

Present research points to the fact that Gordimer is not without solutions to the problem of apartheid. She believed that South Africa could achieve redemption once they got rid of the evil law. For example, she suggests that interracial marriages pave a path towards racial harmony.

Dislocation is a feature of colonization that the author views with understanding. Her language is European and her style is modern, yet her approach to the native subject is humane. Her novels transcend journalistic reporting by creating the imaginary yet convincing plights of immigrants and exiles. The theme of the travails of living in restricted areas in her books is a constant reminder of her disquiet about the living conditions of blacks.

Gordimer's portrayal of binaries, which are an indispensable part of any society, is significant. Because of their coexistence for a long time, one of the binaries tends to dominate the other. Love and violence, loyalty and betrayal, and love and jealousy are some of the binaries that coexist in a human being who is a microcosm of the universe. In The House Gun, the character of Duncan is endowed with the contradictory qualities of love and jealousy. The binaries of yearning for a private life and a public life are present in Burger's Daughter and None to Accompany Me.

The binaries of the oriental and the western, civilized and primitive, rich and poor, men and women, master and servant, liberal and radical, personal and political, and neocolonialism and trade unionism are some of the examples of postcolonial contraries. The binaries of Western Materialism and Oriental Spiritualism are touched upon in The Pickup. The conflict between immigrants and natives is another question. In this novel, only immigrants from poor Oriental nations face punishment in South Africa. The author holds that the South African whites have forgotten their own history. They are all descendents of immigrants. They cannot afford to look down upon the other immigrants.

The author also comments on the implicit acceptance by blacks of their own inferiority. The compliance of blacks in their subaltern position is evident in her characterization of black servants. She does not marginalize blacks' life in her works. Her writings depict the ambitious self-consideration of the colonizer neglecting the welfare of the colonized. Maureen Smales is a typical colonizer justifying the stance of imperialists as benefactors. Women, servants, workers, exiles, ex-prisoners, immigrants and coloured are some of the marginalized sections in South Africa. Gordimer lends voice to the voiceless that live on the periphery.

The author's depiction of South Africa, in its colonial and postcolonial predicaments, perfectly corresponds with the predicament of the Orient. She deals with the emergence of the new bourgeois class of people who ape the colonizers. The dialectic of apartheid leads to a new conflict—between the ruled and the rulers.

Gordimer refrains from providing stereotypical images of Africans. Though she describes the poverty and repulsiveness of blacks' life, her intention is to nail the European rulers as responsible for this condition. Well-meaning characters like Bray and Toby Hood are not hypocrites; they exhibit real interest in the uplift of blacks.

Gordimer exposes the superior mentality of whites in <u>A Guest of Honour</u>. Margot Wentz hints that blacks ought to be grateful to their European rulers for they have ushered in modernity into Africa. Gordimer exemplifies Said's notions of postcolonial theory by pointing out examples of colonial behaviour within the context of Africa. She has proved that the westerners construct the Orient with their power of knowing the Orient. Gordimer does not take the side of westerners. She merely records the sentiments of whites without really sharing the views. Her treatment of the South African subject is not typical of other white writers. She had the courage to break away from the colonialist tradition to perceive truth, to question and to oppose the traditionally held belief that white race was superior.

Gordimer's political intelligence and her epistemological grasp of literary, social and political theories emerge through her books. The writer surfaces as a postcolonial theorist in <u>A Guest of Honour</u>. The dismantling of colonization brings about another set of evil practices like suppression of the rights of industrial workers and women. The postcolonial situation lays bare the inadequacies of the new political system in handling the crisis. The novel also traces how a political party, which originally held aloft pristine ideals, plunges into degeneration after attaining independence. The colonial dialectic works out in a spiral fashion only to unfold the postcolonial dialectic. During colonial rule, the confrontation was between the native and the stranger; in the postcolonial situation, the conflict is between the rulers and the dissenters. In addition, economic dependence on the ex-colonizers paves the way for neocolonialism.

Being above petty prejudices and racism, Gordimer does not nurture a colonial attitude herself. Yet, some of her characters do represent that mindset. White men and women fear their black counterparts. They suspect their servants and spend their energies on safeguarding their lives and properties from probable black burglars. Gordimer has helped her readers perceive the universality of good and evil. For example, one of her characters reminds the readers that the holocaust happened in Europe and that the first labourers in the Industrial Europe spent their wages getting drunk. Savagery, wife beating, and rudeness are not the sole characteristics of Africans alone. The so-called civilized Europeans have exhibited such behaviour earlier.

Gordimer's books demand that her readers approach her with rich schema. Her works are highly literary, replete with references to other great contemporary African and European writers. Comprehension of her works is directly proportionate to the reader's concentration and effort and, of course, his previous literary and critical knowledge. She has a highly objective style that makes the reader feel that she is sometimes too cold to demonstrate any warmth or closeness.

Gordimer's complex, detached and cold style renders comprehension difficult for most of the readers. Some of her works are as inconclusive as a dialectic that does not come to a full circle. A man's story does not end after a conflict. It may leave him in a new quandary.

Move from
Realist novel
to
Consciousness

Though her earlier novels were written in traditional realist mode, beginning with The Conservationist Gordimer has merged different voices and different points of view in her works. Linear narrative is given up in her later works in preference to stream of consciousness technique. Sometimes, the authorial voice intervenes to describe or narrate incidents that happen in another place and time. She ignores the use of speech markers and the conventional 'she said' or 'he said'. The reader has to monitor the conversation closely in order to identify the speaker of an utterance. Sometimes, the reader has to regress in order to decipher the speaker's identity. Characters like Rosa Burger hold dialogues or dramatic monologues in their mind that run to several pages. Her exclusive style is suitable for portraying the lives of her sophisticated and highly literate characters. She has used the method of reversal of situations in a few of her works.

The place in her fiction is mostly South Africa. Sometimes, the scene is also shifted to other African countries. Her characters move to Europe for political reasons or as exiles. The Pickup moves to an Arabian nation and the description of the place is natural and authentic. Whatever be the place or clime, the author is convincing in treating her human subjects.

Gordimer has always presented man in his environment. There is dialectic or conflict at the end of which there is self-realization. She has spelt out that at the end of colonization a situation will emerge where new conflicts will spring up between opposite forces. One conflict is resolved only to give way to another.

Intertextuality is a common trend in her works. Her works have been influenced by other writings as well as by the political events in her country. Incidents happening around were the raw material with which she worked.

Some of her stories fall under the category of initiation stories, which are about individuals coming to terms with the discovery of self. Young men and women such as Toby Hood, Rosa, Will and Hillela attain maturity and adulthood through their encounters with external realities.

A scrutiny of Gordimer's novels leaves the reader in awe as he tries to grasp her outlook. Man and life are the universal and everlasting subjects that she has explored.

Her concern for her people and their issues can be extended to other people in other places. Her service to humanity lies in her support to the human cause wherever it lay. Her objectivity and courage are the products of her hunt for truth. Another conclusion is that Gordimer's political intelligence and her epistemological grasp of literary, social and political theories emerge through her books.

Dialetk

The study also holds that the term dialectic can be applied to Gordimer's works in more than one sense of the term. Primarily, Gordimer has used dialectic as an argumentative device to arrive at truth. In addition, Marxist critics, and the Hegelian philosophers used the term 'dialectic' to mean different ideas. These ideas can also be applied to some of Gordimer's writings.

The unfailing feature of Gordimer's works is humanism. The strands of her different themes are always held together by the unifying theme of truth about humanity. She wrote about the pains and aspirations of blacks were considered as less than human. Her writings are deeply rooted in the social and political milieu of South Africa, yet they are not parochial. After all, marginalization exists in one form or the other in all parts of the world. Wherever her readers hail from, they can relate to the characters and situations they find in her works. Greatness of any literature lies in its ability to make the readers relate their own experience to the fictional experience.

Gordimer's works charted a course of intellectual defence to protect the oppressed races from manipulation and control. The apartheid government had been exercising control over the native Africans in the name of 'separate development', which was, in fact, a euphemism for 'segregation policy.' She had the courage never to stoop to the dictates that originated from the centre. Her individualistic and combative battle against the establishment earned the title "warrior of the imagination." She ranks with artist-activists such as Noam Chomsky and Edward Said who engaged in constructive criticism against the establishment to enable the rationalists to see the truth against the manipulations of the Western rulers.

Further studies can focus on Gordimer's influences, scholarship, narrative techniques and themes. Comparing the author with other African white women writers and men writers might bear rich fruit. The researcher can study her short stories to confirm whether her sympathies are the same in her short stories. Her speeches and non-fiction form a considerable literary corpus on which thematic and stylistic studies can be carried out. Comparative studies with writers of other settler colonies will be useful for comprehending postcolonialism. More research in future will enhance the understanding of the author while stimulating wider readership for the author.

Works Cited

Primary Sources

Gordimer, Nadine. Burger's Daughter. New York: Penguin, 1979.

---. The Conservationist. Harmondsworth: Penguin, 1972.

---. A Guest of Honour. New York: Viking, 1970.

---. The House Gun. New York: Farrar, 1998.

---. July's People. New York: Viking, 1981.

---. My Son's Story. New York: Farrar, 1990.

---. None to Accompany Me. New York: Farrar, 1994.

---. The Pickup. New York: Farrar, 2001.

---. A Sport of Nature. New York: Knopf, 1987.

---. A World of Strangers. London: Penguin, 1958.

Secondary Sources

Abraham, Cecil A. "The Literatures of Victims in South Africa." The Literary Criterion
XIII. 2 (1978): 59-72.

Abrams, M.H. A Glossary of Literary Terms. Singapore: Thomson Asia, 1999.

Achebe, Chinua. "The African Writer and the English Language." Morning yet on
Creation Day: Essays. London: Heinemann, 1975. 55-64.

---."Named for Victoria, Queen of England." Morning yet on Creation Day: Essays.
London: Heinemann, 1975. 65-70.

"American Gets Nine-month Jail Term for Attack on Sikh Taxi Driver." Hindu 21st Apr. 2008: 9.

Anderson, Peter. "Essential Gestures: Gordimer, Cronin and Identity Paradigms in White South African Writing." English in Africa 17. 2 (1990): 37-57.

"Apartheid." Article II of International Convention on the Suppression and Punishment of the Crime of Apartheid. Office of the High Commissioner for Human Rights, Geneva. 1976. 5 Jan. 2008 <http://www.unhchr.ch/html/menu3/b/11.htm>.

Ashcroft, Bill, Gareth Griffiths, and Helen Tiffin. The Empire Writes Back: Theory and Practice in Postcolonial Literatures. London: Routledge, 1989.

---. Key Concepts in Postcolonial Studies. London: Routledge, 1988.

---, eds. The Post-colonial Studies Reader. London: Routledge, 1995.

Ashcroft, Bill and Pal Ahluwalia. Edward Said. New York: Routledge, 2007.

Bailey, Nancy. "Living Without the Future: Nadine Gordimer's July's People." WLWE 24.2 (1984): 215-224.

Barnard, Rita. Apartheid and Beyond: South African Writers and the Politics of Place. New York: OUP, 2007.

Barnouw, Dagmar. "Nadine Gordimer: Dark Times, Interior Worlds, and the Obscurities of Difference." Contemporary Literature 35. 2 (1994): 252-280.

Barry, Peter. Beginning Theory: An Introduction to Literary and Cultural Theory. Manchester: Manchester UP, 1995.

Barnouw, Dagmar. "Nadine Gordimer: Dark Times, Interior Worlds, and the Obscurities of Difference." Contemporary Literature 35. 2 (1994): 252-280.

Berg, Mari-Ann. "Exploring the Mind: Self, Other and Social Context in Nadine Gordimer's 'An Image of Success.'" English in Africa 29.1 (2002): 55-72.

205

Bertens, Hans. Literary Theory: The Basics. New York: Routledge, 2001.

Bethlehem, Louise. Skin Tight: Apartheid Literary Culture and its Aftermath. Pretoria: UNISA, 2006.

Bhabha, Homi K. "Cultural Diversity and Cultural Differences." The Post-colonial Studies Reader. Eds. Bill Ashcroft, Gareth Griffiths, and Helen Tiffin. London: Routledge, 1995. 206-209.

Bharathi, T. "Literature as Political Force: A Critical Appreciation of Gordimer's 'English-Language Literature and Politics.' " The Ravenshaw Journal of English Studies 4. 2 (1994): 19- 27.

Booth, Wayne C. The Rhetoric of Fiction. Chicago: Chicago UP, 1961.

Brutus, Dennis. "Protest Against Apartheid." Protest and Conflict in African Literature. Eds. Cosmo Pieterse and Donald Munro. London: Heinemann, 1969. 95-107.

Carroll, Rory. "Black Men are So Much More Beautiful than White Men." Interview with Gordimer. Guardian 22 May 2003, Comments and Features: 8. 4 Apr. 2007. <http// www.guardian.co.uk. htm>.

Chege, Michael. "Africans of European Descent." Transition 73 (1997): 74-86.

Clayton, Cherry. "Review Article: White Writing and Postcolonial Politics." Ariel 25. 4 (1994): 153-167.

Clingman, Stephen. "The Future is Another Country." Interview with Nadine Gordimer.Transition 56 (1992):132-150.

---. "History from the Inside: The Novels of Gordimer." Journal of South African Studies VII.2 (1981): 65-93.

---. The Novels of Nadine Gordimer: History from the Inside. London: Allen, 1986.

---. "Surviving Murder: Oscillation and Triangulation in Nadine Gordimer's The House Gun." Modern Fiction Studies 46. 1 (2000): 140-158.

Coetzee J. M. "Awakening." Rev. of The Pickup by Nadine Gordimer. The New York Review of Books 50.16 (2003): 4, 6-7.

Collis, Christy. "Siting the Second World in South African Literary Culture." New Literatures Review 27 (1994): 1-15.

Dangwal, Surekha. "The Dilemma of a South African White in Nadine Gordimer's The Conservationist." The Commonwealth Review 8.2 (1996-97): 100-104.

Das, Bijay Kumar. "The Fiction of Nadine Gordimer." Aspects of Commonwealth Literature. Ed. Bijay Kumar Das. New Delhi: Creative Books, 1995. 71-79.

De Kock, Leon, Louise Bethlehem, and Sonja Laden, eds. South Africa in the Global Imaginary. Pretoria: UNISA, 2004.

Diala, Isidore. "Nadine Gordimer, J.M.Coetzee, and Andre Brink: Guilt, Expiation, and the Reconciliation Process in Post-Apartheid South Africa." Journal of Modern Literature 25.2 (2002-2002): 50-68.

---, "Process in Post-Apartheid South Africa." Journal of Modern Literature 25. 2 (2001-2002): 50-68.

"Dialectic." The Oxford Advanced Learners' Dictionary. 7th ed. 1992.

"Dialectic." Webster's Third New International Dictionary of the English Language Unabridged. 1961.

Diouf, Mame Selbee. "Interactions of Race and Gender in Three Black Women's Texts." Diss. U of Kansas, 2006. DAI 67 (2006): 1333A.

Donaghy, Mary. "Double Exposure: Narrative Perspective in Gordimer's <u>A Guest of Honour</u>." <u>Ariel</u> 19.4 (1988): 19-32.

Donge, Jan Kees van. "Nadine Gordimer's "A Guest of Honour": A Failure to Understand Zambian Society." <u>Journal of Southern African Studies</u> 9.1 (1982): 74-92.

Driver, Dorothy. "Modern South African Literature in English: A Reader's Guide to Some Recent Critical and Bibliographical Resources." <u>World Literature Today</u> 70.1 (1996): 99-106.

Dugga, S. Victor. "Insiders and Outsiders: Perspectives of Influences on the Study of African Literature." <u>The Literary Criterion: Special Issue on New Directions in African Writing</u> XXXIV (2004): 5-13.

Eckstein, Barbara J. "Nadine Gordimer: Nobel Laureate in Literature, 1991." <u>World Literature Today</u>, 66 (1992) 7 July 2008 < http://www.questia.com/aboutquestia/about.htm>.

---. "Pleasure and Joy: Political Activism in Nadine Gordimer's Short Stories." <u>World Literature Today</u>. 59. 3 (1985): 343-346.

Eliot, T.S. "Tradition and the Individual Talent." Lodge 71-77.

Ettin, Andrew Vogel. <u>Betrayals of the Body-Politic: The Literary Commitments of Nadine Gordimer</u>. Virginia: Virginia U P, 1993.

Fanon, Frantz. <u>Black Skin, White Masks</u>. Trans. C.L. Markmann. New York: Grove, 1967.

---. <u>The Wretched of the Earth</u>. New York: Grove, 1965.

Forster, Lloren Addison. "The Politics of Creation: The Short Story in South Africa and the United States." Diss. U of Mass., 2007. <u>DAI</u> 69 (2008): 209A.

Gallagher, Susan Vanzanten. "The Backward Glance: History and the Novel in Post-apartheid South Africa." <u>Studies in the Novel</u> 29.3 (1997): 376-395.

Garner, Dwight. "The Salon Interview–Nadine Gordimer." 9 Mar. 1998. 24 May 2007.

    <http://www.salon.com/books/int/1998/03/cov_si_09int.htm>.

Ghorpade, Pradnya Vijay. "Women as Political Activists in Nadine Gordimer's Novels."

    Studies in Women Writers in English Vol.1. Ed. Mohit K. Ray and Rama Kundu.

    New Delhi: Atlanta, 2004. 92-100.

Ghosh, Arpa. "Corpses, Hidden Bodies and Ruptured Discourses in the Novels of Nadine

    Gordimer, Andre Brink and J.M. Coetzee." JSL, Spring (2006): 17-22.

Gilbert, Helen and Joanne Tompkins. Post-colonial Drama: Theory, Practice, Politics.

    London: Routledge, 1996.

"Gordimer Impact." Hindu 23 Nov. 2008, Weekly ed.: 2.

Gordimer, Nadine. "Across Time and Two Hemispheres." World Literature Today

    70.1(1996): 111-114.

---. "Adam's Rib." The New York Review of Books 42.15 (1995): 28-29.

--- . "Bennett Award Acceptance Speech 1986." The Hudson Review 40. 2 (1987):

    182-183.

---. Crimes of Conscience. New Hampshire: Heinemann, 1991.

---. "English-Language Literature and Politics in South Africa." Aspects of South African

    Literature. Ed. Christopher Heywood. New York: Heinemann, (1976): 99-120.

---. The Essential Gesture. New York: Knopf, 1988.

---. "Jump" and Other Stories. New York: Farrar, 1991.

---. The Lying Days. New York: Simon, 1953.

---. Six Feet of the Country. New York: Penguin, 1986.

---. A Soldier's Embrace. New York: Viking, 1975.

---. Something Out There. London: Bloomsbury, 1984.

---. "South Africa." The Kenyon Review 30. 4 (1968): 457-463.

---. "Themes and Attitudes in Modern African Writing." Michigan Quarterly Review IX.

    4 (1970): 221-229.

---. "Turning the Page: African Writers on the Threshold of the Twenty-First Century."

    Transition 56 (1992): 4-10.

---. Why Haven't You Written? New York: Penguin, 1992.

---. "Writer's Freedom." English in Africa. 2. 2 (1975): 45-49.

---. "A Writer's Life: Nadine Gordimer." Interview. Telegraph 4 July 2003. 7 June 2006.

    < http://www.telegraph.co.uk/>.

---. "Writing and Being." Nobel Prize Acceptance Speech. 7 Dec. 1991. 8 Nov. 2007.

    <http://www.nobelprize.org/>.

Gornick, Vivian. "Apartheid's Aftermath." Rev. of None to Accompany Me by Nadine

    Gordimer. The Women's Review of Books 12. 3 (1994): 5-6.

Gray, Stephen. "Gordimer's A World of Strangers as Memory."Ariel 19.4 (1988): 11-16.

---. "A Sense of Place in New Literatures, Particularly South African English." WLWE

    24. 2 (1984): 224-231.

Gray, Rosemary. "Text and Context: A Reading of Elizabeth Charlotte Webster's

    Ceremony of Innocence and Nadine Gordimer's The Conservationist."

    Commonwealth: Essays and Studies, Women Writers in the New Literatures in

    English 13. 1 (1990): 55- 67.

Green, Robert. "From The Lying Days to July's People: The Novels of Nadine Gordimer."

    Journal of Modern Literature 14.4 (1988): 543-563.

Greenstein, Susan. "Apologia Pro Vita Sua?" Nadine Gordimer's "Writing and Being."
Research in African Literatures 28. 2 (1997): 145-153.

Grimes, William. "Es'kia Mphahlele, Chronicler of Apartheid, Dies at 88." New York
Times. 31 Oct 2008. http://www.nytimes.com/2008/11/01/world/africa/
01mphahlele.html

Haarhoff, Dorian. "Two Cheers for Socialism: Nadine Gordimer and E. M. Forster."
English in Africa 9. 1(1982): 55-64.

Halil, Karen. "Travelling the 'World Round as Your Navel': Subjectivity in Nadine
Gordimer's Burger's Daughter." Ariel 25.2 (1994): 31-45.

Hamilton, Paul. Historicism. New York: Routledge, 2007.

Harrison, Sophie. "Nothing Terrible Happened." Rev. of The Pickup by Nadine Gordimer.
London Review of Books 24. 2 (2002): 28-29.

Head, Dominic. "Gordimer's "None to Accompany Me": Revisionism and Interregnum."
Research in African Literatures 26. 4 (1995): 46-57.

---. Nadine Gordimer. Cambridge: CUP, 1994.

---. "Nadine Gordimer (1923-)." 20 Oct 2007. <http://www.litencyc.com/>.

Henley, Ann. "Space for Herself: Nadine Gordimer's A Sport of Nature and Josephine
Humphreys' Rich in Love." Frontiers: A Journal of Women Studies 13. 1 (1992):
81-89.

Hewett, Cami. "Hybrid Marital Union and Healing Apartheid: Nadine Gordimer's
A Sport of Nature." The Atlantic Literary Review 4.4 (2003): 61-78.

Hewson, Kelly. "Making the 'Revolutionary Gesture': Nadine Gordimer, J.M. Coetzee
and Some Variations on the Writer's Responsibility." Ariel 19. 4 (1988): 55-72.

Heywood, Christopher, ed. Aspects of South African Literature. London: Heinemann, 1976.

Honeywell, Arthur J. "Plot in Modern Novel." Kumar and McKean 27-37.

Huddart, David. Homi K. Bhabha. New York: Routledge, 2006.

Huggan, Graham. "Echoes from Elsewhere: Gordimer's Short Fiction as Social Critique." Research in African Literature 25(1994): 61-73.

"'I see stories everywhere': Interview with Zakes Mda." 9 June 2010. www.africultures.com/anglais/articles_anglais/40mda.htm

"In Conversation With Njabulo Ndebele." The Nelson Mandela Foundation speaks to Ndebele. 3 June 2010. http://www.nelsonmandela.org/index.php/news/article/in_ conversation_ with_njabulo_ndebele/

Jacobs, Sean. "The South African Xenophobia." Hindu 21 May 2008, Op-Ed.:13.

Johnson, Karen Ramsay. "'What the Name Will Make Happen': Strategies of Naming in Nadine Gordimer's Novels." Ariel 26. 3 (1995): 117-137.

Jolly, Rosemary. Colonization, Violence, and Narration in White South African Writing: Andre Brink, Breyten Breytenbach, and J.M. Coetzee. Athens : Ohio OH.: University Press: 1996.

---. "Contemporary Postcolonial Discourse and the New South Africa." PMLA 110 (1995): 17-29.

Jones, Eldred Durosimi, ed. African Literature Today. New York: Africana, 1979.

Kaushik, Sreela. "A Woman of Noble Conviction." Indian Review of Books 1.2 (1991): 21.

Kilinski, April Conley. "Embodying History: Women, Representation and Resistance in
Twentieth Century Southern African and Caribbean Literature." Diss. U of
Tennessee, 2006. <u>DAI</u> 67 (2007): 3810A.

Knipp, Thomas. "Going All the Way: Eros and Polis in the Novels of Nadine Gordimer."
<u>Research in African Literatures</u> 24 (1993): 39-50.

Knox, Alice. "No Place Like Utopia: Cross-Racial Couples in Gordimer's Later Novels."
<u>Ariel</u> 27. 1 (1996): 63-80.

Kumar, Shiv K. and Keith McKean, eds. <u>Critical Approaches to Fiction</u>. New Delhi:
Atlantic, 2003.

Lawrence, D.H. "Morality and the Novel." Lodge 127-131.

---. "Why the Novel Matters." Lodge 131-135.

Lee, Hermione. "In Conversation with Nadine Gordimer." <u>Wasafiri</u> 36 (2003): 3-7.

Liscio, Lorraine. "<u>Burger's Daughter</u>: Lighting a Torch in the Heart of Darkness."
<u>Modern Fiction Studies</u> 33.2 (1987): 245-261.

Lodge, David, ed. <u>20th Century Literary Criticism: A Reader</u>. London: Longman, 1972.

Loomba, Ania. <u>Colonialism-Postcolonialism</u>. New York: Routledge, 2007.

Louvel, Liliane. "Nadine Gordimer's <u>My Son's Story </u>or the Experience of
Fragmentation." <u>Commonwealth Essays and Studies: South Africa</u> 14 (1992): 28-33.

Lukács, Georg. "The Ideology of Modernism." Lodge 474-487.

MacKinley-Hay, Linda. "Measuring the Rule: Education in Post-colonial Narrative."
Diss. U of Florida, 2002. <u>DAI</u> 68 (2007): 1470A-1471A.

Mallah, Indu K. "The Ambience of Apartheid." Rev. of <u>My Son's Story</u> by Nadine
Gordimer. <u>The Book Review</u> 16.2 (1992): 30.

Mandela, Nelson. "I am Prepared to Die." Speech at Pretoria Supreme Court, 20 Apr.

    1964. 23 Mar. 2008 <http://www.anc.org.za/ancdocs/history/revonia/htm>.

Marcus, Mordecai. "What is an Initiation Story?" Kumar and McKean 183-195.

Martin, Richard G. "Narrative, History, Ideology: A Study of Waiting for the Barbarians

    and Burger's Daughter." Ariel 17.3 (1986): 3-21.

McAfee, Noelle. Julia Kristeva. New York: Routledge, 2004.

McDonald, Peter D. The Literature Police: Apartheid Censorship and its Cultural

    Consequences. New York: OUP, 2009.

McEvan, Neil. "Outsiders? Nadine Gordimer and Laurens van der Post." Africa and the

    Novel. London: Macmillan, 1983. 128-160.

Monson, Tamlyn. "Conserving the Cogito: Rereading Nadine Gordimer's The Conservationist."

    Research in African Literatures 35. 4 (2004): 33-51.

Morphet, Tony. "Stranger Fictions: Trajectories in the Liberal Novel." World Literature

    Today 70.1 (1996): 53-58.

Morton, Stephen. Gayatri Chakravorty Spivak. New York: Routledge, 2007.

Moyana, T. T. "Problems of a Creative Writer in South Africa." Aspects of South African

    Literature. Ed. Christopher Heywood. New York: Heinemann, (1976): 85-98.

Muhlebach, Andrea. "Between the Fires: Gender and Post-apartheid Reasoning in

    Two South African Novels: Nadine Gordimer's Burger's Daughter, and Miriam

    Tlali's Muriel at Metropolitan." WLWE 36 (1997): 65-85.

Nagarajan, M.S. English Literary Criticism and Theory: An Introductory History.

    Hyderabad: Orient Longman, 2006.

Neill, Michael. "Translating the Present: Language, Knowledge, and Identity in Nadine
    Gordimer's July's People." The Journal of Commonwealth Literature 25.1 (1990): 71-97.

Newman, Judie. "Prospero's Complex: Race and Sex in Nadine Gordimer's Burger's
    Daughter." The Journal of Commonwealth Literature XX (1985): 81-99.

Noor, Ronny. Rev. of The Pickup by Nadine Gordimer. World Literature Today 76.1
    (2002): 115.

Nuttall, Sarah. "Reading, Gender and Nation: Epistemologies in South African Women's
    Writing." Aspects of Commonwealth Literature 3 (1993): 8-16.

Nyman, Micki M. "'But the Test of Absolutely Everything in Life is the Quality of the
In-between:' Subjectivity in Eight Women Novelists." Diss. Saint Louis U, 2006. DAI 67
(2007): 3811A.

Obama, Barack. "A More Perfect Union." Speech. 18 Mar. 2008. 24 Mar. 2008.
    < http://www.msnbc.msn.com/>.

Ogungbesan, Kolawole. "Nadine Gordimer's The Late Bourgeois World: Love in
    Prison." Ariel 9.1 (1978): 31-49.

Oyegoke, Lekan. 'Crystallization of Identity in Nadine Gordimer's Burger's Daughter."
    CRNRL Reviews Journal 1&2 (1995): 55-63.

Parker, Kenneth. "Nadine Gordimer and the Pitfalls of Liberalism." The South African
    Novel in English: Essays in Criticism and Society. Ed. Kenneth Parker. London:
    Macmillan, 1978. 114-130.

Paton, Alan. Hope for South Africa. London: Pall Mall Press, 1958

Pearsall, Susan. "Where the Banalities Are Enacted": The Everyday in Gordimer's
    Novels." Research in African Literatures 31. 1(2000): 95-118.

Peck, Richard. "One Foot before the Other into an Unknown Future: The Dialectic in

    Nadine Gordimer's Burger's Daughter." WLWE. 29.1 (1989): 26-43.

---. "What's a Poor White to Do? White South African Options in A Sport of Nature."

    Ariel 19.4 (1988): 75-93.

Post, Robert M. "Oppression in the Fiction of J. M. Coetzee". Critique 27. 2 (1986):

    67-77.

Quayum, M.A. "July's People: Gordimer's Radical Critique of White Liberal' Attitude."

    The Literary Half-Yearly 36.2 (1995): 41-58.

Ram, Susan. "Adultery and Apartheid." Rev. of My Son's Story by Nadine Gordimer.

    Indian Review of Books 1.6 (1992): 27-28.

Rani, K. Nirupa. "Theme of Conflict in Nadine Gordimer's July's People."

    The Commonwealth Review 4.1 (1992-93): 90-98.

Rao, Radha. "Nadine Gordimer: 1991." Vijayasree 93-95.

---. "Relocating the South African White: Gordimer's Commitment." Vijayasree 96-103.

Reddy, K. Venkata. "'To Read her is to Discover Africa's Realities': Nadine Gordimer."

    The Commonwealth Review 8.2 (1996-97): 90-93.

Rich, Paul. "Tradition and Revolt in South African Fiction: The Novels of Andre Brink,

    Nadine Gordimer and J. M. Coetzee. " Journal of Southern African Studies 9. 1

    (1982):54-73.

Roberts, Sheila. "Sites of Paranoia and Taboo: Lessing's The Grass is Singing and

    Gordimer's July's People." Research in African Studies 24 (1993): 73-85.

Rossouw, Henk. "An Interview with Nadine Gordimer." The Virginia Quarterly Review.

    Nov. 2004. 3 May 2008. < http://www.vqronline.org/webexclusive /2007/

    03/12/gordimer-interview/htm>.

Rowe, Margaret Moan. "Mapping a Way "To Offer One's Self": Nadine Gordimer's

    Burger's Daughter." Commonwealth Novel in English 4.2 (1991): 45-54.

Rudd, Kevin. "Sorry Speech." Sydney Morning Herald. Online Posting. 13 Feb. 2008. 20

    Feb.2008. < http://www.smh.com.au>.

Said, Edward. Orientalism. New York: Vintage, 1978.

Schreiner, Olive. The Story of an African Farm. London: Penguin, 1971.

Schroth, Evelyn. "Nadine Gordimer's "A Chip of Glass Ruby": A Commentary on Apartheid

    Society." Journal of Black Studies 17. 1 (1986): 85-90.

Shinde, Shobha. "Fictionalization of Reality: A Study of Nadine Gordimer's Art."

    The Commonwealth Review 8.2 (1996-97): 94-99.

Singh, Jacquelin. "Prisoners All." Rev. of "Jump" and Other Stories by Nadine Gordimer.

    Indian Review of Books 1 (1992): 28.

Singh, Sri Lalan K. "Racism and Gender: A Study of Nadine Gordimer's Major Fiction."

    Poetcrit 18.1 (2005): 14-19.

Sinha, Shabnam. "Nadine Gordimer: Role as a Woman Writer in a Plural Society."

    The Book Review 16.4 (1992): 26-27.

Smith, Rowland. "Allan Quatermain to Rosa Burger: Violence in South African Fiction."

    WLWE 22.2 (1983): 171-182.

---. "Inside and Outside: Nadine Gordimer and the Critics." Ariel 19.4 (1988): 3-9.

---. "Leisure, Law and Loathing: Matrons, Mistresses, Mothers, in the Fiction of Nadine

    Gordimer and Jillian Becker." WLWE 28.1 (1998): 41-51.

---. "Living for the Future: Nadine Gordimer's <u>Burger's Daughter</u>." <u>WLWE</u> 19 (1980): 163-173.

Smyer, Richard I. "Africa in the Fiction of Nadine Gordimer." <u>Ariel</u> 16.2 (1985): 15-29.

---. "Risk, Frontier, and Interregnum in the Fiction of Nadine Gordimer." <u>The Journal of Commonwealth Literature</u> XX (1985): 68-80.

---. "<u>A Sport of Nature</u>: Gordimer's Work in Progress." <u>The Journal of Commonwealth Literature</u> 27.1 (1992): 71-86.

Sonza, Jorshinelle T. "'My Turn Now': Debunking the Gordimer 'Mystique' in <u>My Son's Story</u>." <u>Research in African Literature</u> 25 (1994): 105-116.

Subbarao C. "The Writer's Conscience: A Reading of Nadine Gordimer's 'The Essential Gesture.' " <u>Indian Response to African Writing</u>. Ed. A. Ramakrishna Rao & C.R. Visweswara Rao. New Delhi: Prestige, 1993. 113-118.

Tarpido, Barbara. "Issues, Not Personalities." Rev. of <u>The House Gun</u> by Nadine Gordimer. <u>The Spectator</u> 7 Feb. 1998: 9-30.

Temple-Thurston, Barbara. "Madam and Boy: A Relationship of Shame in Gordimer's <u>July's People</u>." <u>WLWE</u> 28.1 (1988): 51-58.

Thakur, Nikhil. "Insider / Outsider: A Postcolonial Negative Dialectic on Indo-American Cultural Assimilation." Diss. California Institute of Integral Studies, 2007. <u>DAI</u> 68 (2007): 4877A.

Thorpe, Michael. "The Motif of the Ancestor in <u>The Conservationist</u>." <u>Research in African Literatures</u> 14 (1983): 184-192.

Thumboo, Edwin, and Thiru Kandaiah, eds. <u>The Writer as Historical Witness: Studies in Commonwealth Literature</u>. Unipress: National U of Singapore, 1995.

Tilford, John E. "Point of View in the Novel." Kumar and McKean 287-295.

Toolan, Michael. "Taking Hold of Reality: Politics and Style in Nadine Gordimer."
ACLALS VII (1985): 76-88.

Trump, Martin. "Short Fiction of Nadine Gordimer." Research in African Literatures.
17.3 (1988): 341-370.

Vijayasree, C., ed. Remapping Culture: Nobel Laureates in Literature (1986-1997).
New Delhi: Pencraft, 1998.

---. "Living in the Interregnum: The Case of Nadine Gordimer." Vijayasree 104-109.

Viola, Andre. "The Irony of Tenses in Nadine Gordimer's The Conservationist." Ariel
19.4 (1988): 45-54.

Visel, Robin. "Othering the Self: Nadine Gordimer's Colonial Heroines." Ariel 19.4
(1988): 33-42.

Wade, Michael. "Nadine Gordimer and Europe-in-Africa." The South African Novel in
English: Essays in Criticism and Society. Ed. Kenneth Parker. London:
Macmillan, 1978. 131-167.

Wagner, Kathrin M. "Both as a Citizen and as a Woman: Women and Politics in Some
Gordimer Novels." From Commonwealth to Post-Colonial. Ed. Anna Rutherford.
Sydney: Dangaroo, 1992. 276-291.

Walder, Dennis. Post-colonial Literatures in English: History, Language, Theory. Oxford:
Blackwell, 1998.

Wang, Huei-ju. "Enclosing Others in Cultural Representation." Diss. U of Florida, 2006.
DAI 67 (2006): 2152A.

Weinhouse, Linda. "The Paternal Gift of Narration: Nadine Gordimer's <u>My Son's Story</u>."

<u>Journal of Commonwealth Literature</u> 28.2 (1993): 66-76.

Welty, Eudora. "Place in Fiction." Kumar and McKean 231-246.

Wettenhall, Irene. "Liberalism and Radicalism in South Africa Since 1948: Nadine

 Gordimer's Fiction." <u>New Literature Review</u> 8 (1988): 36-48.

Williams, Raymond. "Realism and the Contemporary Novel." Lodge 581-591.

Winner, Anthony. "Authenticity, Authority, and Application: Buzzati, Kundera,

 Gordimer." <u>The Kenyon Review</u> New Series, 20. 3/4 (1998): 94-120.

"A Writer's Life: Nadine Gordimer." An Interview with Nadine Gordimer. <u>Telegraph</u> 4

 July 2003. 7 June 2006. < http://www.telegraph.co.uk/>.

Yelin, Louise. From the Margins of Empire: Christina Stead, Doris Lessing, Nadine

 Gordimer. Ithaca: Cornell UP: 1998.

Printed in Great Britain
by Amazon.co.uk, Ltd.,
Marston Gate.